Simply the Best

500 football tips for youngsters

Paul Bielby

Foreword by Sir Alex Ferguson

JOHN BLAKE

Published by John Blake Publishing Ltd,
3 Bramber Court, 2 Bramber Road,
London W14 9PB, England

www.johnblakepublishing.co.uk

www.facebook.com/Johnblakepub facebook
twitter.com/johnblakepub twitter

First published in paperback in 2011

ISBN: 978-1-84358-350-9

British Library Cataloguing-in-Publication Data:

A catalogue record for this book is available from the British Library.

Design by www.envydesign.co.uk

Printed in Great Britain by CPI Bookmarque, Croydon CR0 4TD

1 3 5 7 9 10 8 6 4 2

Papers used by John Blake Publishing are natural, recyclable products made
from wood grown in sustainable forests. The manufacturing processes
conform to the environmental regulations of the country of origin.

Every attempt has been made to contact the relevant copyright-holders,
but some were unobtainable. We would be grateful if the
appropriate people could contact us.

About the Author

At five years of age, Paul Bielby was hooked on football. This passion has taken him all over the world as a professional first team player with Manchester United, Huddersfield and Hartlepool and also as a player proudly representing England at youth international level.

Paul's football roles and experiences are quite unique and he now wishes to pass on his tips and observations which have been gathered over the last 40 years and which have brought him both great happiness and some sadness along the journey in this fantastic global game of football.

Paul is currently a former professional player with his own established Football Academy of 15 years called Masterskills Football Academy. He has a UEFA B coaching licence and is a member of the English Football Coaches' Association. Since 1999 he has been a Players' Agent licensed by the English Football Association. He advises and manages professional players and international team managers.

Paul formed the Darlington Primary Schools FA in 1998 and he coaches, manages, sponsors and organises both boys' and girls' competitions and also district teams in northern England.

He is also a motivational speaker in business, universities, colleges and schools. Paul was recognised for his work with children and young people in July 2008 when he received the MBE from Prince Charles at Buckingham Palace in London.

Contents

Acknowledgements

To my wonderful parents, Arthur and Grace, who gave me love and support.

To my wife Christine and our lovely children Michael and Helen, who share their dad's passion for football.

To the youngsters, parents and coaches at my football academy who have so enthusiastically and energetically given me the inspiration to write this book.

To Tony, Jackson, Rob, Barry and Gareth who love this fantastic game and provide young people with the opportunity and freedom to display their talent.

To the many wise, wonderful and inspirational people I have met in the last 40 years in football, business and friendship who I have had the good fortune to meet and who I have had the pleasure to listen to and learn from.

Foreword by Sir Alex Ferguson

In my time as manager of Manchester United and previously at Aberdeen, I have recognised the vital importance of the role played by parents and coaches in encouraging children and young people to enjoy this wonderful game of ours.

Paul Bielby was a young professional at Manchester United in the 1970s when he made his first-team debut as a 17-year-old in the red-hot atmosphere of a local derby against Manchester City at Maine Road. Quite a start for a young player.

At this time he also represented a successful England Youth team which won the European Youth Championship. The team included Bryan Robson, Ray Wilkins, Glen Hoddle, Peter Barnes, Alan Curbishley and Dave Jones. Not a bad team!

Paul's book *Simply the Best* describes his appreciation

of his four years at Old Trafford and also his ups and down experiences at Huddersfield Town and Hartlepool United.

His experiences and his many and varied roles in football make this book an interesting must read book for youngsters, parents, coaches and teachers who wish to inspire, motivate, and give confidence to boys and girls of all abilities.

Paul highlights the need for children to develop a healthy and happy lifestyle, and describes how children learn and what makes a good coach for youngsters at grassroots level. He enlightens the reader on the skills required to improve young players and coaches and then shows the checklist of skills that clubs are looking for in the better performers.

To really grow as a player Paul focuses on tips to improve both football fitness and football mentality and the vital support that parents play in their youngsters lifestyle and football path.

Paul's love and passion for football shines through in this book and he has immensely enjoyed developing, encouraging and motivating youngsters at his own football academy. He knows how to bring the very best out of children and young people and his tips will maximise the football experience for everyone.

In 2008 Paul's work in grassroots football was recognised when he received the MBE from Prince Charles at Buckingham Palace.

I am happy to recommend this book and pleased that Paul has agreed to make contributions from his profits to Cancer Research UK and to the Sir Bobby Robson Foundation.

Sir Alex Ferguson
Manager of Manchester United Football Club

Introduction

One of life's great sights is seeing a youngster either taking part in their chosen sport, watched by encouraging and admiring parents, or happily eating their sweets as they support their favourite football team with their soccer-mad dad.

I was hooked on football from the age of four, when my dad took me to the park for a father-and-son kickabout. The smell of newly-mown grass always transports me back to those exciting days spent with my hero – my dad.

At primary school we played four-a-side in a small dingy gym while avoiding the piano in the corner and the stacks of chairs surrounding our small 'pitch'. The feeling of scoring the winning goal against the prone bench was exhilarating.

These football foundations led me to captain the school team at 10 years old – which felt as good as when I received the MBE from Prince Charles at Buckingham Palace in 2008 aged 51!

As you read on, I hope that my tips and observations trigger special memories in your footballing history. These experiences can play an important part in the life of children and youngsters and encourage them to enjoy their football to the maximum.

At 10 years old I witnessed England go crazy when we won the World Cup in 1966 and felt the national pride as we displayed the red, white and blue colours. The scene was set and I was captivated by this beautiful game.

Street football was played by children of all ages for hours in those days, until we received the dreaded call from our mums – 'Tea's ready!' Match over. Kids played with a sense of freedom and without any adult supervision or interference. We practised our skills and allowed ourselves to make unquestioned mistakes while practising the dribbling skills that George Best displayed as he snaked down Manchester United's wing at Old Trafford.

It was a surreal moment when I eventually joined Manchester United and at 16 years old I was invited to occasionally join the first-team squad – including Bestie – at the Cliff training ground.

In ability terms I wasn't good enough to tie his shoelaces – who was? But for two seasons I did a decent job as his apprentice, keeping his Stylo boots immaculately clean.

Following County success at secondary school I was scouted by Leeds United and met the manager, Don Revie, who tried to persuade my dad that Leeds United was the club for me. However my team were Manchester

United and after meeting the great Sir Matt Busby, Dad and I were chuffed to bits (that's an understatement) when Sir Matt said that he wanted me to join them.

I was so driven and dedicated to doing well at Old Trafford and I was rewarded with a first-team debut at 17 years of age in the cauldron-like atmosphere of Maine Road against local rivals Manchester City in front of 51,000 highly charged fans.

Representing England at Youth level and winning the European Youth Cup in Switzerland in 1975 was a highlight which proved to be the height of my achievements as a player.

Most of my life in football has been a great joy, working with youngsters to develop their skills and persuading them to make football a big part of their lives. My enthusiasm remains as strong as ever and for the last 13 years I have split my football life between my Masterskills Football Academy and my work as a football agent licensed by the English FA.

We are a nation that goes ballistic whenever our sporting heroes are in sight of winning competitions, and football has the ability to lift us out of our sometimes mundane lives when our jobs are not motivating us or we have problems in our private lives. Football is powerful.

Look how our national flag suddenly comes out of hiding and we display it proudly in our windows and cars – we even erect flagpoles in our gardens to show our commitment to our team and country.

You have a great opportunity to make a difference in the life of a child. The observations and tips in this book will help make football more enjoyable for you as a parent, coach, teacher or referee and will provide a great motivation for your young players.

This is a book that everyone who loves our great game can easily understand; it will confirm things that you are doing really well and show areas where you can improve. The book suits all abilities from the young boy or girl just starting out in football to the teenager at a club academy who is hoping to make a career as a professional player. It will show how you as an adult can do well in junior football and even start your own Football Academy. It will be a useful read for school teachers, and you will realise the great job that referees do. There is also a chapter showing why the gifted players need an agent and why some clubs do not want them to have one.

If you have the passion and the enthusiasm to still learn and be open to new ideas you will enjoy reading the 500 tips and observations. From this book new ideas in your mind will be created and you will become a better coach or player.

Enjoy the book and enjoy the journey. Take in all the highs and work through the few lows.

If you have a football story to tell or just want some advice regarding school football, Junior club football, setting up your own academy, being a coach or you are just looking for an agent for a gifted player I look forward to hearing from you. I might even publish your story one day! My e mail address is p.bielby@btinternet.com

Paul Bielby

The Path Forward

This book is split into 15 sections, which you can dip into at any time. It is aimed at both boys and girls – women's football is currently enjoying huge growth.

I will show you how a youngster learns from a very early age and how this great game can have a positive effect on their whole lives. Your relationship with your child can really develop through football and this book will hopefully inspire you to help out and possibly even coach your child's junior team or even start up your own football academy as a business.

You will see how skills and techniques are developed, and how to choose a junior club for your youngster so that they can begin to learn the art of teamwork.

I will show you what football scouts are looking for in terms of ability, attitude and mental strength.

You will see how your personal skills as a coach can be

enhanced, which will make you even more popular as a coach or as a teacher at school.

Football is such an up-and-down game of fluctuating emotions and passions and this book will show you how to deal with any problems that might occur in this sport where everybody seems to have an opinion.

I will show you how gifted and elite youngsters can develop the mental toughness which the players at the top of the sport have acquired and the need for focused, 100% dedication to succeed.

Nothing is More Important to a Parent Than the Health and Happiness of Their Child

Not many parents and grandparents would disagree with that statement. Ask any parent the same question and without exception they will confirm that nothing is more important in life than the health and happiness of their children. Think back to that moment when you found out that you were going to be a mum or dad. Think of the warm joy you experienced sharing the news with your parents and family and the smiles you received when your friends and work colleagues were given the great news.

Planning ahead to the birth and wondering if the baby is a bouncing healthy boy or girl is an exciting time. But while my wife was focusing on the colour of the baby's clothing and the style of the baby's room, my thoughts drifted to the day when I would buy the child's very first football strip. Dads think like that, don't they!

Go Puppy Go!

Compare your child to a healthy and happy puppy dog. If the puppy is given love, a good meal, bags of praise and an opportunity to run, jump and play with a ball then watch its tail swish from side to side. It's the same experience with your children – they need freedom to play, twist, turn, roll over, run and jump.

All you need to do is add a football to the mix, create a goal out of jumpers and coats and you have the base to take your relationship with your child to another level.

Do not think that this is a sport only for dads and little boys to participate in. Mums are finding that this basic football activity with their sons and daughters is a fantastic way of bonding with their loved ones.

Girls' and women's football is one of the world's fastest growing sports and that is set to continue. Girls see traditional male-led sports such as football, rugby and cricket as an exciting and very attractive alternative to traditional women's sports such as netball, hockey, gymnastics and dancing.

Kids love it when mum and dad play sport with them, and you just have to see the pleasure in their faces when they tell their friends of their parents' participation. While our children are so precious to us, are we restricting their playtime activities because we fear of them getting injured? Can you remember the thrill and the sense of freedom you enjoyed when you climbed trees, played in the park and stayed out until Mum called you inside?

Children love the time they spend with their parents and they also love the freedom of playing with their friends where they experience the life skills of getting on with people, inventing their own rules, keeping score and even arguing about fouls, free kicks, corners and penalties. They experience the thrill of winning and the disappointment of getting beaten. The more they get used to these events the more they learn about life – after all, much of adult working life is about winning and losing.

Making Football and Sport an Everyday Activity and a Way of Life

Have a real think about this one. The positive work you do with your children when they are very young will influence them and stay with them all of their lives.

Imagine that because of you, your child will have adopted a healthy attitude to taking part in regular sporting activity. Let's face it, football is a massive global sport played and watched by millions of children, youngsters and adults every week.

Encouraging your youngster to be active and to follow football as their chosen sport will give them stronger muscles and bones, they will be leaner and – if their sporting activities are combined with eating sensible food in healthy portions each day – their body fat will be controlled and they will be less likely to be overweight.

This could be a great legacy to your children as they could eventually persuade their children, who could then persuade their children, to have happy sporting lives. And so it continues!

The knock-on effect of having a child who enjoys football, takes part in football and through playing and practising their football skills is that they will develop a positive outlook. They will sleep better, have a confident manner about them and will be better equipped to deal the everyday challenges that occur.

CHAPTER 1

What Children Want

1. They want love and support from their parents, brothers and sisters, grandparents and family. Lets face it, isn't that what we all crave for at any age – somebody to love and somebody to share our good times and those times when the unexpected happens totally out of the blue?

2. They want to be listened to by their parents. Children do not just want to receive gifts and presents and then be left to play with them alone; they want to play, talk, smile and laugh with parents and enjoy their hobbies and pastimes. They want to tell their parents about the good things that are happening in their day.

3. They want to have their own friends to play with. Children love to enjoy the company of children their own age and share their interests and hobbies. They want to feel part of a team which they are at home with their parents and brothers and sister, they are at school with their schoolmates and teachers and they will be in future years when they start to play team sports.

4. They want to have a comfortable home life, with their own room, or to share with their brother.

5. They want to receive praise and compliments which will boost their confidence and self esteem. We know as adults that daily events in our lives can either really boost our confidence and happiness, or send our emotions the other way. To receive even the simplest compliment, pat on the back or thank you can do wonders and children will respond to this boost in a very positive way.

6. They want to be active, take part in activities and enjoy being part of a team. Children have tremendous energy and enthusiasm when they are fully engrossed in an activity that motivates them. When they share this activity within a team environment they learn that hard work, thought and teamwork is vital if they are going to be the best or win the event.

While we welcome Child Protection and Health and Safety rules I believe that we have become a society that is wary of taking part in sporting activities. Previous childhood pastimes like playing outside have been replaced by children staying in and playing with computer games. Our children are being restricted and mollycoddled and it is not good for them. For me, all the fun of being a child was in being outside and doing the physical stuff like playing football, playing hide-and-seek and climbing trees. We are so much more reserved and cautious now.

7. They want to feel fit and healthy. Seeing the joy and vitality of children running, jumping and enjoying life with their parents or pals is one of life's great pleasures and to adult it brings back memories of times when they were having similar fun at a similar age.

8. They want to enjoy their food – with the occasional treat. At a time when supermarkets are giving ever more space to ready meals, burgers, cakes, biscuits, chocolate, sweets, ice creams and sugar-filled drinks it is important that you give your children food they like, but food that is also good for them. They will copy what you eat, so why not help all the family and only bring in the house food that is good for you? Of course everyone needs an occasional treat, but we should try to limit these to maybe once or twice a week.

9. They trust their parents to provide them with rules and discipline. Rules surround us every day and most of the time we don't realise it, as they are habits in our everyday life. We have a time that our employer wants us to start work and a time to finish work; it is same with children at school. Children subconsciously need rules. They need to know what is allowed and what is not, what is acceptable to say and what is not, and they need to learn good manners, respect and compassion for their fellow human beings. Children can be gradually given more responsibility and the freedom to voice an opinion. It is important that children are made aware of people who are perhaps not as fortunate as they are, perhaps due to ill health or poverty in a developing country. This awareness will help them appreciate what they have, and not crave things that they do not really need.

10. They want to have the freedom to express themselves and to experiment in low-risk circumstances. If children are not allowed to have the freedom to make mistakes they will not learn anything or develop a mind for flair and invention. Life would be boring if we all had the same personalities and abilities. Look at a child face when they have worked something out by themselves. The surprise on their face when you say well done you worked that out for yourself is a picture.

11. They want to play with their parents, brothers and sisters and enjoy events such as family gatherings, going to sporting events, the cinema and theatre.

WHY FOOTBALL?
12. Because it's a universal game with huge participation around the world played by both men and women as children, youngsters and adults.

Billions of people tune in to see football being played on TV and they are attracted by its glamour and the attractiveness of the sport – they want to see football being played in front of full stadiums projecting a lively vibrant atmosphere.

13. Football is a simple game to set up and you need little equipment to start playing. You can play with mum and dad and your pals and you only need a football and jumpers for goals.

14. It's a game played in virtually every school playground, with very noisy enthusiastic youngsters. Surveys confirm that children who play sport on a regular basis achieve higher grades in school and better behaviour records.

15. Football teaches discipline, how to keep fit and feel part of a team, it's character building and teaches the life skills of learning to win, draw and accepts defeat. Football is one of the best ways to develop a child's creativity and imagination.

16. Football is a healthy activity, keeps kids fit and they experience the camaraderie of being part of a team. Research has shown that children who are physically active have improved social skills and self esteem. Instil the habit early and it could last a lifetime.

17. Football is great for bringing kids and parents together to share their hobby and passion. It creates conversation topics and debate on football teams and individual favourites.

18. Football builds children's conversation with their pals and they love buying and swapping football cards of players and teams.

19. They'll grow to like a football team – it's usually Dad's favourite and they love to wear their team's kit with pride.

20. Football shows us how to win, lose and draw and I must say that I have made long-lasting friendships with parents whose children were in my teams.

21. Football is passionate, obsessive game that involves us in wide ranging emotions of ecstatic happiness and low despair. Football is in our spirit and it reaches those parts that other sports can not.

WHAT CHILDREN WANT FROM FOOTBALL

22. They want to have fun! Football can deliver many things that children want in life. Watch the faces of children and adults when their favourite player in their favourite team scores a goal. Watch their magical enthusiasm when they play and score a goal – the effect is priceless.

23. They want to play football with only the very basic rules and without the pressure of being told off by adults for making mistakes. This is a massive point.

24. They want to have the experience of feeling the freedom to experiment and try new skills to run with the ball and to score great goals from great shots.

25. Children these days are told 'It's the taking part that counts' – it is as if they should apologise for trying to win. However, in the real world life is very competitive and it *is* about winning and losing. Through sport, children learn to enjoy the great thrill that winning brings and this feeling motivates them to improve.

I always loved to win games and to make or score goals for my team. Children enjoy the buzz that winning gives them and they learn that in winning you need to play as a team. I learnt from a very early age that I could not win without the combined efforts of my team-mates.

While winning was exhilarating, I also had plenty of practice at losing and the experience of winning and losing gave me a balanced view of life and I grew to understand that providing I always gave my very best and I still lose then I could do no more. Always applaud effort.

26. When children score a goal or win a game they want to openly celebrate with their mates and show great enthusiasm doing it. They watch television and copy the goal celebrations of their heroes, even though they sometimes do not know the story behind the players' unique celebration.

27. The key to children enjoying their football and improving is the praise and positive feedback they receive from parents, spectators, coaches and particularly from their team-mates. This is probably the most important point in this book. We all thrive on praise, a pat on the back and a 'well done'. Praise gives us energy, lifts our spirits and we have a desire to do more. People like people who give out genuine praise. It is a fantastic thing to do in your life and it makes people happy which hopefully you love to do.

28. It is always interesting to see a player seek out a parent when they have just scored a goal, or contributed to making a goal. Parental approval is very important to them. That is what kids want – fun, happiness, winning games, variation, feeling fit and healthy, receiving praise and feedback. That's the recipe for success.

OBESITY: THE THREAT

As adults we know how easy it is to put weight on, but how difficult it is to lose that weight when we want to. Health experts have been trying to prompt governments to act to improve our health, and especially in the last few years when the potential obesity problem has been highlighted. When you read the next group of observations and tips I hope that you see the power of eating the correct foods which help shape your individual lives and those of your family. Your family is so precious to you and therefore you must take notice of the type of food and the quantity of food you are all taking in.

29. An estimated 400 million people in the world are obese, with 20 million of them being under five years old. The condition raises the risk of diseases such as type 2 diabetes, heart problems and cancer and may cause problems in the bone joints and knee areas.

In England, health experts are stating that the figures show that we are the middle of an obesity epidemic and that the cost to the National Health Service will be vast. Youngsters in inner cities are particularly prone to obesity, and children who have overweight parents are more likely to be overweight themselves. Overweight children run a high risk of being an overweight adult. Being physically active and eating the correct sized portions of the correct food will provide the foundation for a happy life.

Alarmists are stating that a generation of children is so obese that they may not live beyond the age of 50. The cost of being overweight will affect our clothing costs and visits to the dentist, chiropodist, doctor and osteopath.

Obese and overweight people have less chance of a happier life, getting jobs, of attracting social respect and have a much lower level of self esteem. Obesity is when we are more than 20% above our standard weight for our height.

30. The time to stop this epidemic is now, in early childhood, when eating habits are formed and before obesity causes the symptoms that raise the risk of heart conditions and diabetes.

Parents are responsible for giving their children a great start in life and there is no better way than to start them off on the right food while educating them that a fit, healthy body will provide them with a fitter happier mind. Stopping obesity means preventing it happening in the first place.

31. Children of parents who are or were obese themselves are much more likely to be overweight themselves. An overweight child is likely to become an overweight adult. Overweight children can be embarrassed about how they look in sports kit, and because of this they often try to avoid taking part in sport. But by not taking part the problem simply as they don't get enough exercise and their weight goes up. This chain reaction can then cause problems such as a lowering of confidence and self esteem and sometimes even depression.

32. Studies have highlighted that people who eat quickly until full are three times more likely to be overweight. The research concludes that people should eat slowly and in calmer surroundings, which will help them digest their food better and they will then eat less.

33. 25% of 13–17-year-olds in England are obese compared with only 11% in Germany and only 10% in Holland. The number of children needing hospital treatment in the UK for obesity has doubled in the last eight years.

34. Since 1993 up to 5,000 school playing fields in England have been sold off. There are fewer sports lessons at primary schools in particular, where the pressure to improve the achievement statistics in reading, writing and mathematics has taken important time away from the physical education timetable.

35. Fast food consumption has soared and there is more space given in supermarkets to highly profitable cakes, biscuits, jams, crisps and sweets. The more these products are purchased by the consumer, the more space they are given in store. Food manufacturers are encouraged to develop new products with a bigger range of varieties, sizes and flavours. This sector also produces a high level of in-store promotional activity to encourage sweet-toothed purchasers into increasing their sugar intake.

However, if you want all the fantastic benefits of being the correct weight, feeling really healthy and full of life, giving up or reducing the amount of fast foods and sugar-laden treats you eat is a very small price to pay.

36. Parents can lead by example in a number of ways. Firstly, we know children are influenced by their parents so make sure that you as a parent are not overweight yourself. Your children will copy many of your habits and actions so throw out all those fatty foods you have in the kitchen cupboards, fridge and freezer and buy in healthier foods that will provide the daily calories you require but will not put on further weight. You and your children are now on the right track to lower your weight and maintain a new you.

Next, start walking a lot more than you normally do. Forget the car and the bus and start walking the kids to school. Gradually you will find that you are walking a lot more in a week than you did before. Write down your walking mileage per week. If you walk quite briskly for 20 minutes, that's about one mile. Give yourself some fruit as a sweet reward for your efforts. Start the process now.

You'll find that you and your youngsters are bonding even more now as you have a mutual goal that you can work at together – getting fit and eating healthier. In a few weeks you will be feeling healthier, slimmer and less sluggish and your mind will become sharper. I promise you it works.

This is now work in progress and you have done the hardest bit which is getting started. The burgers and pies and chips have gone and you have lost the taste for ice cream, chocolate bars, biscuits, cakes and fizzy pop. Don't worry, they haven't left your life forever, but now they are just an occasional treat.

Believe me, you and your children are now forming new habits which will open up a new life for you. You should be proud of yourself – your confidence should be higher and your self esteem raised.

37. As you now start to feel alive and your weight has reduced, what about trying to play a sport? Starting at a lower basic level and progressing will give you the confidence you never thought was possible. Have you noticed how well you are sleeping now? Try kicking a football around in garden or the park with your youngster, have a laugh, fall about in the mud and score the type of goals that you see your footballing heroes score on the TV. After this energetic kick around, a shower or a bath will make you feel great. Refresh yourself by bringing water into your life. Drink water before and after exercise and, if you can drink 6–8 glasses of tap water per day, watch how your skin improves and your weight comes down again.

38. Lead by example and be active. Plan outings with your family and monitor the time that your youngsters spend watching the television and playing on the computer. Try and make sure that when your child is eating a healthy low-fat meal you are not eating a more attractive but unhealthy dinner.

39. I hope that you take heed of the warnings from the world's health experts, that your child has the fitness to enjoy their football, and that you live a long and happy life so that you can marvel at their energy, enthusiasm and happiness. You will receive a school report commenting on your child's academic work, but do they give their opinion of your child's health? Teachers are in a position where they can compare children in terms of their intellectual and social skills, so why not comment on their health? In the future a child's report might include the child's BMI (Body Mass Index), highlighting the child's perfect weight for their height and advising parents on the best food and exercise for each individual child.

Helping potentially overweight children early will prevent them from further exaggerating the problem and also making them happier human beings.

Your children love you with a great passion and they need you all of their lives. If you are not motivated to eat healthier, maintain your correct weight for yourselves then do it for your children. They want happy lives and happy parents, and they love you so much.

HAVE A FOOD PLAN
40. If you do not put oil, water and the correct fuel in your car and you forget to blow up the tyres, the car will not

work. It's the same with human beings. If we do not eat the correct balance of food at the right time, and in the correct portion sizes, we will not function correctly. It is a very simple comparison but it does make sense.

41. Healthy eating starts in the home. Children will watch what you eat, how you eat and how much you eat. Give children small meals but often. Children thrive on a happy variety of foods.

42. As a parent this is one of the most important decisions you will make in your life. If you teach your child which foods are healthy for them, and when and how much to eat, they will feel good in themselves and have much more confidence in their appearance.

43. Healthy eating is the key thing – ensuring that children are neither underweight nor overweight for their age and height. It is important that children have small meals, but often. Children will thrive on foods they enjoy and if this includes bread, pasta, rice, noodles and potatoes as well as fish, chicken, turkey and only the occasional red meat, together with healthy portions of vegetables and fruit, then they are eating a good cross-section of healthy foods that will boost their energy levels.

WHICH FOOD IS BEST AND WHEN?

44. We are bombarded with people telling us what to eat, asking us who we would like to eat it with, and of course all the celebrity chefs are showing us how to cook it. We need the correct food to give us energy, make us grow, allow our bodies to repair themselves and to keep us in good health.

45. Our bodies function best when we take in the correct amount of carbohydrates, protein, fibre, vitamins and minerals. Getting the balance right gives us the energy to perform well in our daily activities.

46. A calorie is a unit of energy that food gives the body. It is important that that we do not eat more calories than we burn off. If we do this then we will put weight on. This doesn't mean that you have to spend all of your time studying the backs of food tins and packets to check the ingredients, but it is a good idea to have a general idea of what is good and not so good for you.

47. Carbohydrate-rich foods give us energy and these foods include bread, cereals, rice, pasta and potatoes. Both adults and children need carbohydrates which provide the body's most important source of energy, and eaten in the correct amounts give us the foundation of good health.

Carbohydrates are broken down into two types: sugars and starches. It is better to eat more of the starchy carbohydrates .The sugars provide a quick blast of energy and include jam, honey, fruit, cakes and biscuits. The starchy carbohydrates include vegetables, pasta, rice and cereals, but these foods also contain proteins, minerals and vitamins.

48. We all need fibre to move the food through the digestive system and vegetables and fruit provide this function.

49. Protein is important to healthy growth. Poultry, meat, eggs, fish and dairy products such as milk and yogurts provide nutrients which are key to healthy growth. Much of our body tissue including skin, bones and muscles are made up of protein which aids repair and growth.

50. Calcium is great for healthy teeth. Milk, yogurt and cheese play an important part in healthy teeth and gums.

51. Fats are also an essential part of our diet, as they are our main source of energy when we are sleeping and resting. Fats help keep our skin healthy and keep us warm. There are two forms of fat: saturated and unsaturated. Unsaturated fats are better for you. Saturated fats – which can raise your cholesterol – are found in foods like butter, cream, milk, meat, cheese, biscuits and chocolate. As high cholesterol is dangerous to your health these are the products to eat in moderation. Healthier unsaturated fats are found in fish, corn, nuts and soya beans. Cholesterol is a fat-like substance which is in our blood. This can build up in our artery walls and, if unchecked, can cause circulatory and heart problems.

52. Vitamins help our bodies to work efficiently. As with proteins they help in the repair and growth of our bodies tissues. Vitamin A helps our sight and tissue repair, Vitamin C helps beat viruses and heals wounds and Vitamin D helps achieve healthy teeth and bones.

53. To maximise our children's energy levels we need to feed them at key times of the day and these obvious times are at breakfast, lunch and dinner. Having meals at these key times of the day are vital to replenish our energy reserves and boost our enthusiasm levels.

54. Experts tell us that breakfast is the most important meal of the day and it's easy to see why. Eating a good breakfast really does set you up for the day. In addition, many people believe that it is not good to eat a meal after 8pm as it can affect the digestive system and can cause interrupted sleep. When we get out of bed in the morning we have probably not eaten any food for 10 hours. That is why breakfast is important to re-energise your mind and your body.

55. A good breakfast to get your child ready for school and sport could include cereal with chopped fruit on top, eggs on toast or simply toast with a preferred spread. Perhaps leave a fry-up of bacon, eggs, sausage, tomatoes and baked beans for a very occasional treat as it is very high in fat – and you could try grilling bacon and poaching eggs instead of frying them to lower the fat content.

56. It is a good idea to check with your child's school to see an example of the menu offered to the children who have school meals. If it is healthy then all well and good, if it is not healthy then it might be better to give your child a packed lunch with a sandwich, a piece of fruit and a bottle of water or milk. Perhaps you and other parents could persuade the head teacher and school governors to adopt a healthier approach with a healthy menu.

57. At teatime, give your family fish or lean chicken with a variety of salads and vegetables, or a pasta or rice dish with a sauce and some lean meat. A bowl of strawberries or mixed fruit would go down well as a dessert. In my job as a football agent I once had lunch at Manchester United's Carrington training ground with Sir Alex Ferguson, and all the players finished their meal with Jaffa cakes.

The meeting with Sir Alex gave me an insight into his methods of man management, and how he keeps his staff and players 'grounded' and normal. In other words, he does not like bigheads but team players and an 'all working together' mentality.

I had been to the French Under-17 Championships to see a striker called Julian Vial. Julian was regarded as the best player for his age in France. I travelled 1800 miles to see him and he only touched the ball three times–but he did score three goals! At the Carrington lunch Sir Alex sat us down in the canteen but there were no knives and forks laid out. Sir Alex apologised and brought us some cutlery. He also saw that we had no water and glasses so he again went to get them for us. Julian's father was surprised and said in his French accent, 'Sir Alex he is a servant'. I think that Sir Alex's message was to show them that everybody at Manchester United helps out in a family atmosphere.

58. To keep portion sizes sensible, it could be a good idea to try using smaller plates and bowls. Let the children stop eating when they feel that they have had enough, as asking them to eat it all up could make them feel bloated and sluggish.

Children's food preferences can become habit-forming from early childhood so it is good to give them a good healthy variety start from the start. Try to keep chips or fried foods as a rare accompaniment to a meal. A good alternative could be a salad, corn on the cob, or baked beans which are an excellent and low-cost alternative.

59. Pre-school children have smaller stomachs so small, regular portions of high-calorie meals are the best option. Make meal times a happy occasion and after their main meal resist the temptation to give them a sugary dessert and instead let them choose a piece of fruit.

60. Fruit and vegetables are shown in every dietary plan put together by the professionals and the recommendation is that everyone should eat at least five portions of fruit and vegetables every day. However the statistics show that this is not the case as 20% of people do not eat any fruit in a week; however 80% of people will eat chocolate, crisps and biscuits in the same period. It is always a good idea to have fruit readily available and on view in the house as it will provide a healthy snack to satisfy the tastebuds.

Bananas are a favourite of sportspeople around the world as they are packed with the sugars which provide muscle energy. Watch the top tennis players and golfers as they snack on a banana in the middle of their respective competitions. The sugars in foods like bananas and other slow-release carbohydrates assist muscles to use energy. Bananas are also welcomed after sport as they replace the glucose that was burned up during the activity.

61. Scientists are increasingly telling us that our attitudes and behaviours can be affected by the foods that we eat. Try changing the food habits of an unruly youngster by taking fast food, sweets and fizzy drinks out of their lives and replace them with healthy alternatives containing less sugar. You will see a noticeably big improvement in their attitude and demeanour.

DRINK UP – LOTS OF IT

62. Water is quite simply the best and most readily available drink to keep you functioning and it makes up around two-thirds of your body weight. Professional footballers are virtually attached to a bottle of water throughout the day – they recognise the benefits.

63. If you feel thirsty and your lips are dry, you are already in the early stages of dehydration. What you have perhaps not realised is that being thirsty also reduces your energy levels. The thirstier you become the more lethargic you will feel. Be aware of your energy levels and top up regularly with a glass of water.

64. Youngsters have a greater fluid requirement than adults as their body temperature regulation is lower than adults'. So they need more fluid top-ups. Particularly watch youngsters in hot weather as they sweat more and therefore need more water to replace the lost fluid.

65. I remember my grandma telling me as a child to drink six to eight glasses of water a day, which would give me the energy to think, run and to keep my skin healthy and my organs functioning correctly. How right she was.

66. Water intake is a vital component of footballing performance and a shortage in a player's body will affect concentration and muscle movement and leave the player exhausted, severely dehydrated and, in hot conditions, potentially cause heatstroke. Energy levels, strength and co-ordination will be affected by dehydration and additionally players are at more risk of being injured if they are dehydrated.

Some players even start a game in a dehydrated condition and consequently appear lethargic and lazy. Before every activity make sure youngsters have a drink of water.

67. It is important that parents, coaches and teachers are aware of a youngster's water intake and ensure that they provide regular drink breaks. If a player does not like normal water, add a little juice. In a match players need water before, during, at half-time and after the final whistle.

68. If a child's water intake is good, they will feel good and continue to perform both mentally and physically. Parents should note that if a child's sporting performance and mental school work is dipping it could be that they need to drink more water over the course of the day.

If they are feeling light headed, have a rapid heartbeat or their mouth and lips are dry they need topping up with water immediately. Teachers and sports coaches should know the signs and how to prevent dehydration.

69. As with food, children will watch how much water their parents and other adults drink and will copy. So make sure that water becomes a normal everyday part of your life, and make it obvious that you as an adult like water. Show them that you are drinking plenty of it.

70. Put a jug of water on the table at all meal times, and give children a bottle of water to take to school and additional water to take to sporting and social events. On a hot day at a sporting event there is a good chance that the drink you brought along could end up being drunk before the event has even started. Make sure you bring extra supplies, or take some money with you.

71. Water is so much healthier than sugary drinks such as fizzy pop and it is easy to change a person's preference to water when they see and feel the benefits that changing to water brings. Fizzy pop has no place at sporting activities, especially for the players taking part. If a player drinks something fizzy before or during a match, they will feel bloated and will quickly need more to drink as the high sugar content will make them even thirstier.

72. Too many fizzy drinks, coffee and tea can cause headaches, make it difficult to concentrate and can also disturb sleep, so the values of swapping these for water are positive.

73. A high number of injuries take place in the last ten minutes of a match and it is no coincidence that at this stage of the game players are more vulnerable to dehydration.

SMILE

74. Have you noticed that when children smile it makes us happier people? It's especially true when that child is ours. Smiling children light up our world, and make us adults feel that we have contributed to their happiness.

75. Imagine if your child went through life with a happy, smiling demeanour. It would create a fantastic knock-on effect for you, your family and your child's friends. People are attracted to happy people and people with a positive outlook are very popular with colleagues at school, college, university and in the workplace.

76. Smiling produces and releases feel-good hormones and levels of the stress hormone, called cortisol, are lowered when we smile. Smiling helps you feel in control and relaxed, and it lowers your blood pressure.

77. The effect that football can have on a child's happiness level is extraordinary. It is as if a whole new exciting world has opened up for them to share with their friends, brothers and sisters and the rest of their family.

78. Being part of a football group at school, at an after school football club, a Sunday morning junior team or simply having a kick around with their pals is one of life's great pleasures. Watch the youngster smile and laugh when they score a goal – or when a pal falls over or misses a sitter of a chance to score!

79. Smile, laugh and enjoy life – because you are unique on this planet and being happy and making others happy will enrich your life and boost your popularity.

HAVE A NAP AND RELAX

80. With all the enthusiasm and energy your child puts into their football, and hopefully into their school work, they are going to need adequate rest and quality sleep.

81. Rest doesn't have to mean sleep – it can actually mean that they take up another hobby, go on holiday, visit the cinema or go and watch a sporting event. In other words, rest can mean anything that will take their mind off football, or the pressures of school work, for a short time.

82. Sometimes there is nothing better than simply putting our feet up on the sofa and having a nap for 20 minutes or so. It works for me as I then feel invigorated with an immediate surge of energy. If I have a nap for more than 30 minutes I can wake up lethargic and a bit grumpy. Monitor how long is best for you and your child.

83. While we as adults need 7–8 hours' sleep per night, growing youngsters function better with 9–10 hours per night. If you feel that they are having a bad day and are a bit moody and tetchy then there is a good chance they need more sleep – and possibly more water to drink.

84. Rest is essential for our bodies to recover, both physically and mentally. A healthy sleeping pattern will ensure that children perform better at school and in their football activities. Properly rested children are more positive, happier, mentally sharper, more relaxed and can concentrate better and for longer periods of time and they are more likely to deal with any difficult situations that might arise.

Rest is essential for our bodies to recover both physically and mentally. Lack of sleep equals a loss of energy and we lose concentration more quickly.

GET YOUR KIT ON – THAT'S THE DIFFICULT BIT!

85. Sometimes the toughest part of exercise is a mental hurdle – actually getting our kit on, lacing up our trainers or football boots and walking out of the door.

86. As you get ready, recall how you feel when you return home after training and enjoy a hot shower or a steaming bath. You have probably had a laugh and a joke with your team-mates, and enjoyed the thrill of being part of a group and the success you encountered when the skills you tried worked and your team came together to enjoy a positive result.

87. Imagine leaving the changing room after training with the lads. You feel invigorated, with a healthy glow and a sense of achievement. Your muscles are relaxed, your skin feels good and your confidence has been topped up because you have worked hard and contributed to the team.

88. Your appetite is good and you even seem to enjoy your food more. You now know you are less likely to suffer heart attacks, lung disease or arthritis and with each training session your cholesterol is being kept at an acceptable level. Knowing this, how good do you feel?

89. Simply getting your kit on and getting out there has many benefits and it has no doubt made you feel happier and even a bit younger. Yes, this exercise lark has many benefits and the more you do it the better you feel.

HOW A YOUNGSTER LEARNS

90. When kids fall in love with football, they have unlimited enthusiasm and a great passion to be involved, to learn and to improve. They have a desire to practise and improve their skills and they love to play football with their parents and their pals. As a child I loved watching football matches with my dad and I was in awe of the top players as they performed their inspirational skills. Give children little objectives, such as practising different turns with the ball, or ask them to see how many 'keep ups' they can do. Children enjoy achieving objectives as long as you make the task attainable. Children, youngsters and adults who are enthusiastic want to do more, not less.

91. Children and youngsters thrive on praise and this positive feedback energises them and they practise even more. The very best footballers throughout history had a desire to improve their skills and they practised in every spare minute to perfect their technical skills and style. Gifted players such as the great Brazilians of the past, or the present-day flair players such as Ronaldo and Messi, have worked tirelessly to develop their wonderful technique.

92. With encouragement from parents, kids will watch football on the TV and attempt to copy their new heroes. Children visualise the skills they see when they're playing in the park or training with their team. They are influenced by seeing great players and fantastic goals but sometimes they can also copy the negative side of football, with players diving and intimidating referees. This negative copying must be stamped out early in a child's development as it can slow down the fulfilment of everyone's objective, which is to improve skills and techniques.

93. Quality practice and repetition is the key to improvement and if children attend a recommended after-school academy, their skills and techniques will improve. They will learn the basic fundamentals of controlling the ball, looking up and the skill of accurate passing with the correct speed or pace on the pass. They will learn that good teamwork is vital to produce consistently positive results.

94. Parents have a great influence over their children and in the majority of cases a youngster will support the same team as their dad. This sees the youngster start to wear the team strip and then eventually the national team kit with their favourite player's name emblazoned on the back of their shirt. The youngster and his football-mad family enjoy their country's appearance in the European Cup or World Cup especially when they fly the countries flag from the flagpole in the garden or the car when it is decked out in their team's colours.

95. Young players are enthralled and hypnotised when they go to watch their favourite team play for the first time. They see the stadium from the outside and the enthusiasm builds until they climb the stairs and see the hallowed immaculate green turf for the first time. The smell of the newly mown grass, the buzz of the crowd, and your favourite sweets, what more could a youngster want?

This experience is magic and they watch with great interest, noting the skills and hopefully taking this experience into their next training session. This phase sees another bonding between dad and lad.

There is a chance though that you are taking Junior too early. I took Michael, my then five-year-old son, to his first match and when he wanted to leave at half-time, I asked him what he enjoyed the most and he said his sweets. When asked 'what did he like most about the match' he said 'the police horses chasing the men off the pitch were funny'! Not the first impression I had hoped for but now at 26 years old he loves his football with a great passion.

CHAPTER 2

The Growing Years

THE EARLY YEARS

96. From birth to five years old is a wonderful age where personalities start to develop. Football dads can't wait to start kicking a ball around with Junior and the child's whole football experience must start positively, with Dad giving lots of praise. Go overboard with your praise and they will repeat the action to receive more praise. Maybe leave him little notes saying how well he is doing.

97. The interaction between father and child is priceless and seeing a dad falling over and diving about in the mud trying to save Junior's shot at goal will bring great joy to you both, especially if caught on camera or video camera. The video camera was one of the best luxury items I have ever bought. As a family we look back and see our son and daughter 20 years ago when they were six and four years old. The laughter and joy it gives us all is brilliant and the memories of seeing our four parents, who have now passed away, are invaluable.

98. Cherish every minute you spend playing football with your child. These precious times can eventually lead to him or her joining a junior club and you could quite easily become involved as a secretary, coach or manager. The years fly by incredibly quickly. Keeping a diary of your children's events is good to look back on and recall those fun activities.

99. A male authority figure is so important in the life of a youngster, setting guidelines in terms of behaviour and displaying signs of a caring nature. In primary schools women account for over 90% of teachers and I believe some boys are missing out on having a positive male role model in their lives, especially if they have no dad living at home.

There are great opportunities for young men to study to be a primary school teachers, and if they have a love of general sports and maybe even some coaching awards they will be welcomed on board by most schools. They say there are few jobs for life, but teaching could be one of them. Children will think you are fantastic for giving them a sporting opportunity.

CHILD DEVELOPMENT: 1–2 YEARS OLD
100. Start your football relationship with Junior from as early as one year old. Why not? They are walking now so good luck, go for it, get the video camera ready and enjoy

your magical football journey which will give you both memories to last you a lifetime. But don't waste your time looking for coaching books for one- to four-year-olds as none have been penned yet.

101. Give them a tennis ball and practise placing the ball in and out of their hands while give them an approval smile. Go down to their level on the floor or grass clown around and encourage mutual laughter. Throw the ball a short distance and encourage them to bring the ball back using their hands. Can the child stop the ball with his hands? Support your child underneath his arms and put their foot on the ball. In the same position, push their foot to kick the ball and show great enthusiasm and praise. A child's attention span is very short so it is up to you to add the motivation. Short bursts of 10 to 15 minutes are enough, maybe twice a day.

CHILD DEVELOPMENT: 3–4 YEARS OLD

102. Research shows that three- to four-year-olds in Britain spend 80% of their waking hours immobile as their parents fail to ensure that they have enough physical activity. That is an appalling statistic. It is important to plan a couple of hours of playtime at different times of the day to give them happy, healthy movement and exercise.

MOVEMENTS WITH THE BALL

103. If a child is not active at this age they could be inactive throughout their lives. If this is the case, start today and get them moving now and with patience and you will be delighted with the results. Wow, what an opportunity to put your child on the correct track to healthy activity. It can be achieved by working out a plan of who will play with Junior, when, and what activity will he like the most. Experiment and see which one appeals most.

104. Reward them with a ball sack, which is an indoor football similar to a beach ball but smaller and made with a cloth exterior. It is lightweight and safe to kick inside the house. If you can not find a ball sack, try rolling socks together to make a good-sized ball – but move valuable and ornaments out of the way for safety!

In good weather encourage outside play in the garden or park and use a small lightweight size 2 or size 3 ball. Encourage the child to trap the ball with each foot in turn and try 10 traps with each foot.

Look to teach good style and technique in passing. Buy some small flat cones and show your child how to pass the ball successfully and repetitively though two cones at varying distances. Make sure that this activity is achievable for your child, and that success is praised. Occasionally kick the ball away and encourage them to dribble the ball back to you using both feet. Put six cones in a line and tell them to dribble in and out of the cones using both feet. You practise it yourself and tell Junior that he is much better than you.

Children love to run so give them 10 seconds to race with the ball in and around the cones, again making sure that they achieve some success on most occasions.

The idea is to catch your child being successful and then

reward them with their favourite drink (not fizzy pop) or a piece of fruit – or why not buy a star chart so that each time your child does well he can stick another star sticker on his personalised star chart.

I remember when I was in the Manchester United youth team we had a star chart where one player received a 'man of the match' star in training and matches and you got an 'assist' star if you made a goal. It really gave us focus. It also made sure that the maker of the goal was given just as much praise as the goal scorer. The players loved this idea and it kept motivation high. At the end of the season the ones with the most stars won trophies.

The parents of tennis players Venus and Serena Williams made them practise their sport from a very early age. Imagine them hitting thousands of golf and tennis balls until they developed a good style and technique. Football is the same. You can start your child off in football making sure that they have the right style and technique. Then encourage them to practise receiving and controlling the ball and accurate passing and positive shooting. Imagine then what could be achieved if they practised their new-found skills hundreds and thousands of times.

Practise five days per week for 10 minutes only. Keeping it short will help their concentration and stop them getting bored. However, if they really enjoy practising, why stop them? Fun and enjoyment must always be the motivation for them. Give them regular big hugs and tell them you love to play football with them at every opportunity.

105. Children at this age need activity and should not stay inactive for long periods. They need at least 20 minutes of physical activity per day and this should include run around games to include agility, co ordination and balance, which will help keep them fit and supple. To mentally stimulate them they need to play with their favourite games and toys.

106. Children love to please their parents and they crave attention at certain times. Try to invent activity games that you all can take part in and maybe even buy music and sporting keep-fit DVDs that can keep you fit – Junior might also be encouraged to jump and move around too.

At this great age kids become very interested in adventures and in vigorous activities and taking part gives them a great feeling and releases tension and boredom.

CHILD DEVELOPMENT: 5–6 YEARS OLD

107. This is a key age for parents to spend time with their children and if parents show little enthusiasm for the child's interests, the child can develop behavioural problems just to get their parents' attention. I occasionally see lovely children who are slow to react to my coaching instructions or who are doing things that they usually wouldn't do to gain my attention. It is not children being intentionally naughty but its normally happy children with different events happening in their lives. I discreetly try to find out the cause of their new behaviour and usually it's a parent break up or them not receiving the attention at home that they need.

108. The swarm is the norm. 'Spread out!' shouts the coach as the five-year-olds chase the ball all over the field. Don't be too concerned about this as it is natural and normal. At this age, kids have no idea of spatial awareness and why should they? Children at this age are only concerned about their own performances and not their team-mates'.

Any criticism is hurtful to children at this age. In their minds they want to get involved and they want to kick the ball, so they go and chase it. When they reach the ball first they just kick it anywhere (some even pick it up). Very rarely will they lift their heads up and accurately make a pass to their team-mates. If they do control the ball and look up, their decision-making isn't properly developed yet so one of the swarm is likely to win the ball from them. They are just so pleased to be involved with their mates and they love to do what all children do at this age which is run jump, fall over, get up, roll over, fall over again, smile, have a laugh and, yes, fall over again!

109. Gentle persuasion will encourage them to spread out, look up and occasionally pass the ball in the correct direction to a team-mate. In a training session they need a lot of varied activity with each activity lasting no more than 10 minutes as their attention span is still short. Tailoring the activity to their language abilities and way of thinking will really help them understand the sporting objective, so a bit of clowning around and over-exaggerating a goal celebration will keep them online to continue to enjoy their football.

110. Give children very simply instructions and keep it short, but always give a couple of demonstrations to make sure they understand. Children love it when you tell them that the training they are taking part in is exactly the same as professional footballers'. It is true – except that the training is tailor-made to their age and abilities. Although at this stage the children are very young it is important that discipline is maintained to maximise all of the players' enjoyment. Awarding a 'good performance' sticker after each training session, or a player of the month certificate, will focus their efforts to achieve, and assist with concentration.

111. Children love to play matches and their first introduction to being in a team provides great fun for them and great entertainment for you. The best match format is four-a-side as the players receive a lot of the ball and they have turns at defending and attacking as the ball moves around quickly on a very small pitch. When they put the coloured bibs on and are given the name of a famous team they feel elated with excitement.

During these loosely structured matches, some of the children's minds will wander and parents will sometimes question Junior's involvement when they see him looking everywhere except at the ball, being completely static, or hardly chasing the ball like the other players. What the parent hasn't seen is the player's involvement with the ball in the training session before the match.

Two to three ten-minute matches will satisfy the children's needs and, provided the rules are loose and relaxed and adults are not shouting at them to do this or that, they will be hungry to come back for more.

A good habit is to encourage the players to shake hands with their team-mates and opponents after the match's. Tell them what the final score was and that you were really pleased with them. Make sure that they have water to drink and that a bath or shower is taken when they arrive home.

CHILD DEVELOPMENT: 7–8 YEARS OLD

112. This for me is the group that naturally shows the most enthusiasm for football. They are at that age where they feel more grown up and they have left the 'babies' behind. They are so lively, with bags of energy. It is important to tap into this energy and to give them the same enthusiasm in return. Let them play within a very light structure. If you are putting on a shooting, passing or a one-on-one session, give them a very brief one-minute instruction with a demonstration and then step back and just watch their honest endeavour and sense of fun. It is fantastic to watch. Again, discipline will be required, but do not quell their enthusiasm.

113. Youngsters at this age are now starting to enjoy watching football on the television and occasionally going to live matches. They will start to mention not only the best players in the English or Scottish Premier Division but also teams and players from the cream of European and world football. Their attention span and concentration are improving and they are beginning to understand the rules of the game. They now ask more questions and they have a thirst for knowledge.

This is a key time to learn and useful information is being stored in their memory. This is a good time to reinforce major points that you want them to practise. Parents, teachers and coaches can have a major impact on their future as they are in the magic stages of learning and can be influenced on their future thinking.

114. They now enjoy competing and they like to work out how they can win matches. They love praise and they start to enjoy watching other players' positive skills. They begin to understand the basic tactics of spreading out on the pitch, not always chasing after the ball and looking up to see their team-mates. They begin to understand that working together as a team is important to win matches.

115. They now have a team to support, a player to idolise and they start to support their country with a passion. They want to wear the colours of their heroes and they will closely watch how the players conduct themselves on and off the pitch. They will discuss football with their pals and like adults they will debate football transfer rumours and forthcoming matches and results. They start to understand branding and take an interest in which sports companies make which trainers, football boots and team kit. They now know how much a pair of boots costs and even which football icon wears which brand. Their birthday and Christmas presents are dominated by football equipment. They now start to understand how a league table works and how many points can be earned for a win or a draw.

116. Physically, at this age children's muscles are strengthening and their range of movements including agility, balance and co-ordination are improving. When the children arrive at a training session you can see that their stored up energy is about to be unleashed. They have probably been in a classroom all week and they are ready to explode into action.

A good start to training would be to put them in a tag session, obstacle course or running and sprinting competitions, where they want to know which team has won. If a team has cheated and not completed the sprints correctly, tease them half way through and tell them in two minutes you will tell them which team has been disqualified. The look on their faces will be so funny and it starts the session on a fun note.

117. Action is very important to them and they want to know the score in their training matches. They like to win rewards such as player of the month of man of the match awards. This is a good time to encourage them to practise at home using cushion control to kill the ball dead and practise keeping the ball up. They can now train longer as their stamina and strength is improving and they start to understand that repetition and practise will help them improve. For the last thirty minutes of a training session the children will want to play matches, and the best format to ensure that every player has many touches of the ball is four-a-side on a small pitch of 30 x 20 yards. All the players can take turns to be goalkeeper and they will all have the opportunity to score goals, defend, tackle, pass and practise their dribbling. Play with very loose rules and keep the game continuous with no interference. This small game is not only for the young players as professional players love to play this format in training as it keeps every one involved.

THE INFLUENTIAL YEARS

118. Between six and 13 years of age it the time of learning and experimenting. Children like to have some independence. Their personalities are starting to shine through and they love to play more aggressive and competitive sports. They start to copy their parents' behaviour and interests. If parents show a lack of interest, children will begin to get their parents' attention in other ways which may include bad behaviour. Between six and 13 years of age a father has a major opportunity to influence his youngster. Youngsters need a positive caring environment at home and school where they are happy to develop their personalities, and skills in a calm atmosphere.

119. As junior football clubs and out-of-school activity groups become more popular it is important to place good male role models, such as teachers, sports coaches in their path to confirm to them the positive aspects in life that you have taught them. In this sometimes difficult stage of life kids need good role models to show them how to praise other people, show kindness and also how to achieve a disciplined atmosphere with a sense of humour. I have found in my football academy that children who receive little praise in their lives try to be naughty or a nuisance just to bring attention to themselves. I actively look to find them doing something so that I can praise them. When they receive this praise you can see them mellow and glow with pride and start to enjoy the activity as all the others do. They sometimes give the impression they are not bothered but once they receive praise you can see it means a lot to them. This pat on the back boosts their confidence and self esteem and it is then that their natural pleasant personalities start to come through.

CHILD DEVELOPMENT: 9–11 YEARS OLD

120. The biggest asset a player of any age can have is enthusiasm and this age tends to produce the most excitable players. They love practising skills, and they interact and make friendships with their team-mates. Their personalities and characters are now opening up and they are developing an opinion.

121. Their decision making in small-sided matches is improving and they will start to pass the ball more accurately and consistently with an improving pace on the pass. They have stopped chasing the ball and they have now started to lose their marker and find space. They are learning the basics of defence and attack and understanding different positions on the pitch and the relationship between positions.

They understand that there is a reason for lifting their heads when in possession of the ball and they know that the hardest working team will usually win the match. Their team-mates are now more important to them.

122. Players begin to understand that if their style and technique is good, they will improve and have success. They will learn that if they control the ball without it bouncing off them, it will make them look good and this will further grow their confidence and eagerness to improve further. They will see that with practise and repetition their control, passing, shooting and heading accuracy will improve.

123. This is a great age to further enhance their movement and motor skills as they are moving into the age group where they love to learn new skills and techniques. Coaches will see big levels of enthusiasm in setting up competitive sessions of mini circuit training which includes co ordination, balance, agility, speed and flexibility. A smooth running style can be achieved by repetitive sessions ironing out jerky unbalanced movements and turning them into a style of 'pleasing to the eye', fluid movements which include better use of the hands and arms. The correct arm movements can make the player move and appear faster and boost their confidence to run at players in matches.

124. This is the age where some players are hoping to achieve a place in their primary or junior school football team. The school will have trials and then once the team is selected will play matches against other local schools or they might venture further a field and play in district or county football. If your city or town or district has a representative team the best players from the primary or junior schools will be asked to attend for trials. Some have teams for boys and for girls.

CHILD DEVELOPMENT: 11–14 YEARS OLD

125. As the child moves from primary or junior school, where they have been the oldest, they are now sharing assembly time with 16-year-olds. This is quite a significant jump in their lives and after a few months you should see a maturing in their attitudes. They have gone from being the big kids to being the little kids at secondary school.

Starting a new school and meeting new people can be both exciting and daunting. To a sports-minded youngster the move can be uplifting, as sport at this level can be seen as more important as you now have a number of male and female sports specialists which primary schools do not provide. The sports facilities will be much better and the range of sports available will be far greater. Joining senior school could be the first step a child makes into making a career out of working in sport. Obviously they would need to work just as hard on the theory part of sport as on the practical side. However, there are very good working opportunities in many aspects of sport from becoming a professional player to training as a PE teacher, sports development officer, physio, events manager or sports psychologist. Janet Leife, a friend of mine, moved from being a very experienced Sports Development Officer in her local council to a position as Events Manager with Cancer Research UK organising Race for Life events throughout the United Kingdom. She loves it.

The range of sporting opportunities jobs is excellent. As we all have to spend 40 hours a week at work, why not work in a job that you enjoy and one that really motivates you?

126. This part of a youngster's life is when the major growth spurt starts. It is basically when a child's bones grow, and it can be a difficult time – a youngster is growing and also seeing their bodies and their friends' bodies showing major changes. Their minds are also developing and maturing and they are not sure if they should act and behave as a child or as a mini-adult.

127. Adults need to be aware that the youngsters need help and support to get them through these teenage years. It's a good idea for parents to sit their children down and tell them about puberty before it happens. This way they won't be as shocked as they could be when the changes arrive. The adolescent growth spurt starts in girls from around nine years old and in boys from around ten years old. Reassurance is needed to show them that these changes are normal and that their friends will go through the same changes, perhaps a little earlier or a little later. At this delicate stage adults must be positive with any comments, as youngsters can be cruel and openly comment on their friends' or brothers' and sisters' body changes. Young people who are not seeing their bodies grow at the same rate as others of their age need to be given reassurance that their changes will happen soon too.

128. Young footballers and sportspeople now need to ensure that they eat the correct foods to support this new growth. As growth speeds up, their bodies need more calories and from around 11 years old more calcium is required to help the growth of their bones.

129. As the growth spurt and puberty starts, children's height will increase and this is followed by a weight increase. In girls this rate of growth slows at 13 years old but they will continue to grow until they are 18 years old. In boys, growth slows down at 15 years old but continues until they are 19. We are all different so these guides are within a year or two. The big weight changes usually occur in girls at 13 and in boys at 15.

130. During this growth spurt you could well see a change in your child's co-ordination and they could look a little 'leggy', which can make their movements look ungainly and awkward. At this stage they can also look a little lazy so it's a good idea to work a lot with the ball – you can still provide them with a lot of stamina work but they won't realise it as they'll have a ball at their feet. Once the player gets used to their larger body and it starts to feel more like a natural fit, they can move forward positively.

131. We must all understand that eating the correct food is our fuel which provides us with energy. The key to giving the adolescent teenager the energy required is that parents monitor their food intake. Milk is a great drink to provide calcium and fish, meat and poultry will provide iron, with tomatoes, broccoli and strawberries and oranges providing vitamin C. Good daily portions of vegetables with their main meals, followed by a piece of fruit for pudding, will really satisfy their growing bodies.

132. Sporting activity is as important as the correct food during these years and a combination of both will make them happy people. They will then enjoy their schoolwork as they will be mentally sharper and more alert, have fun with their fellow adolescent friends and sleep well in the extra hours they tend to need as they get used to the growing bones.

133. Football is such a universally popular activity which provides all the vigorous, athletic movements that youngsters need. It will help to encourage your youngster to take part in football if they have a friend sharing their enthusiasm to take part. Try them with both five-a-side and full 11-a-side matches to determine which one they prefer. There is a likelihood that they won't be quite as good as older players or players who have been involved in team football for a number of years. It wouldn't really work if you put a youngster in a club or team that had been together for a long period of time. Their initial enthusiasm could wane if they find it a struggle and hardly receive a kick of the ball.

It's always good to find your level. It would be better to be a regular starter in a Division 3 team than on the subs bench for most games in Division 1!

134. At this age the youngsters start to feel closer to their pals, as their shared growth gives them even more things in common. This new physique that they are growing into arrives at a similar time as sexual maturation and support from parents, as well as friends who are going through these same changes can be a great help during this unsure time of their lives. Traditionally, parents have found difficulties in explaining 'the birds and the bees' to their children and have left this task to schools and finding out from their friends. It is one thing being told that this will happen to your body but another thing experiencing it, as changes gradually occur.

135. Parents can feel that their opinions are now being questioned more, and their youngster will now have a developing personality that can occasionally seem confrontational. Parents can understandably think that their child now has a 'know-it-all' attitude and that they are difficult to reason with. Stay very close to your children and understand the changes taking place in their lives. Gradually allow them more freedom – as long as they know that they still have to adhere to the discipline that you have put in place as their guardians and loved ones. You are still a role model for them; you are the still the ones they truly love and you have supported them all throughout their lives to this point. As a parent you are quietly helping them to have a common sense approach to life and helping them make sensible decisions that will eventually make them happy young adults who have a positive impact on other people they meet in their lives.

136. At this age, youngsters are now changing to 11-a-side football and many dads and coaches wonder how the kids will cope with the offside rule and how to explain the Laws of the Game to them, never mind putting it all into practise. Keep it very simple. Around 18 months before they are due to start 11-a-side matches ask them to watch games on television and to focus on players being caught offside. Children love to copy and coaches can start phasing the offside rule into small-sided games in training. Give all the players the opportunity to play in defence and attack and they will get used to the offside rule more easily than you think.

As you probably won't have people on the touchline giving offside decisions it isn't realistic to expect the referee to get every offside decision right on every occasion. Generally, if it was monitored, you would see that the good and bad decisions are evened out in a match or during the season.

137. Players are now starting to understand the individual positions on the pitch, and particularly the position that they enjoy playing in or being asked to play in. They are also starting to understand how the positions come together in a team formation. They know that to do well as a player and as a team that they have to compete strongly for the ball, especially at the start of a game to confirm to the opponents that your team is 'up for' the challenge. The players know that a 'we are together' mentality is preferred to a 'me me me' mentality which will win nothing.

At my three professional clubs we were always told the

same thing just before we went out to compete: 'Win your individual battles all over the pitch'. Effort is always a taken-for-granted basic requirement of every professional player.

PLAYING POSITIONS

138. Now they are moving to 11-a-side, players need to learn their new positions and it is important to make it simple for them. Play 4-4-2 and do not change formations. The following points show the physical and mental requirements each playing position requires.

Goalkeeper: Good handler of the ball, agility, brave, tall, gets in line with the ball, quick reactions, kicks well off the ground and high and long out of their hands. Shouts instructions and directs defence.

Full-backs: Play right-footers at right-back and left-footers at left-back. Good passer, strong in tackle, quick, enthusiasm to join in attacking movement. Works well with the central defenders. Good fitness.

Central defenders: Strong, dominant, good header of the ball, loves a tackle, a winning personality. Good passer of the ball. Does not want to concede goals. Quick.

Central midfielders: Good ball control with good first touch. Accurate passer with good vision, has good mobility, and has endurance and fitness to get up and down the pitch. Strong tackler with a determined personality. It is good to have a defensive-style central midfielder and an attack-minded central midfielder. The defensive one will play in front of their own defence and break up opponents attacking play and the attacking central midfielder will link up with their forwards and wide players and try to score goals. An attacking midfielder has the flair and creativeness to open up defences with a variety of skills. Midfield is known as the engine room in football – generally if these two players play well the team will play well. Need grit and determination to succeed in this position.

Wide midfielders/wingers: Attack-minded and quick. Good dribbling skills, good crossers of the ball, can score important goals. Will also be prepared to track back and tackle.

Strikers: The goalscorers. Good shooting and heading technique, ability to hold the ball up until team-mates support them. Usually one big aggressive striker plays with one smaller but quicker and more agile striker. Controlled aggression. Determined to with stand strong defensive tackling. Confident finisher and just loves to score goals. Positive mentality, they will continue to try to score even if many previous attempts have failed. They play with great enthusiasm.

Substitutes: A player who wishes he was playing and being involved right from the start. Needs to be ready as they might be called upon at any time. Will most likely appear on the pitch in their strongest position so mentally they need to rehearse the position and be ready to make an instant impact. Are you a striking substitute who has a record for being a super sub? This type of quick player can take advantage of tired defences with their refreshed energy and athleticism. They must anticipate a mistake from a weary defender or goalkeeper.

139. When we mention a skilful player in football we tend to think about the flair players who create and score great goals. All players on a football field have skills and the most overlooked skill is of the big aggressive central defender who has stopped opponents scoring through his aggressive tackling and heading. He has been brave enough to dive in and block many goal bound shots. He might not have displayed the tricky silky skills of a dribbling winner who has crossed for your striker to score the winning goal but he has been the strong foundation stone to give your team the opportunity to win the game with his physically strong skilful display. Thank your winger and your striker for providing and scoring the winning goal, but it could have been the players in the team that did the aggressive part that you should thank most. This type of rugged player is a must in any successful team.

Once a coach has helped players to feel comfortable in their individual roles he will then help them bond together to produce attractive passing football when they have the ball and a 'get it back quickly' mentality, when your team have lost possession of the ball.

140. Players in this age range will have fewer touches of the ball in matches now as there are 22 players on a much bigger pitch. They will need to learn to be more disciplined in their more rigid positions. They will play matches of 25 minutes each way and, as a player in a full 90-minute match only touches the ball for just over two and a half minutes, they will only touch the ball for about two minutes each game or even less. This means that they need to learn what to do in the 47 minutes of a 50-minute match when they do not have personal possession of the ball.

They will understand the importance of playing as a team to win matches and the philosophy of it is 'we' that wins games and not 'me'. They will listen to a respected coach who gives them easy to understand simply instructions that work, is patient with them and who recognises their strengths, far more than their shortcomings.

As they learn their position in the 11-a-side team their decision-making will improve and with match experience they will start to get it more right than wrong. The more they get it right the more quicker they will start to make the correct decisions. This knock on effect will then help their confidence which will encourage them to work even harder to improve.

PLAYER DEVELOPMENT: 14–19 YEARS OLD

141. Well here we are, well and truly in those growing years! Testosterone levels in boys lead to larger bones and a big increase in muscle size. You will have heard about these years from other parents complaining about difficult, moody young people who are lazy, who will not do anything to help around the house, who sleep in until lunch time at the weekend and who answer back far to often.

Stop moaning, parents, because that was you at their age and they do not have your experience of life yet! You know you love them to bits and you would do anything for them. This is where you as a parent, or as a teacher or football coach, can really help to guide them through this unique but uncertain stage in their lives.

142. Players are growing taller and stronger as they reach adulthood, which assists them in meeting physical challenges. They now have a much better understanding of their strengths and weaknesses and the positional roles they are asked to take on. They love competition and their need to become successful and win games is more important to them. Coaches who support players at this age gain their respect.

143. Parents and their offspring can clash as the young person is now developing an opinion, and wants that opinion to be heard. Young people can test an adult's patience by trying to go beyond the house rules such as arriving home at an agreed time and doing household chores.

144. Football can play a big part in bringing teenagers safely through this period and parents, teachers, coaches, managers and team-mates can create a fantastic environment where everybody is equal and where everybody can bond together, share experiences and provide a high level of support.

A caring parent will make sure they know where their youngsters are on an evening when, understandably, they want to socialise with their like-minded friends. Parents should know who their children's friends are and whether they are suitable characters for their son or daughter to socialise with. Many intelligent youngsters have lost their way by being part of the 'wrong crowd' and they can be led and influenced by others who do not have the parental support that you give your children. It can mean that these youngsters do not focus on their school work, and consequently they do not achieve the exam grades that their true ability and hard work would have given them. Many in later life regret this mistake and go back to take their exams, but for others they have missed the window of opportunity.

When youngsters see caring adults giving great praise and attention to them they become calmer, and they relax knowing that the characteristics this age displays is understood and that they are receiving encouragement and praise. A football coach for this age group must be supportive and kind but must however still maintain discipline and ensure that everyone acts within the club's code of conduct.

145. Short and to-the-point training sessions work best at this age. Skill sessions with the ball are preferred with shooting and one-on-one or two-versus-two followed by small-sided competitive games of two-touch football or normal matches. The best training session would also include a fun warm up, stretches, and also at the end a cool-down and more stretches. 70 or 80 minutes would be perfect with only a short two-minute debrief at the end. At this stage long-distance running is to be discouraged, as are long lectures from the coach.

146. As this age group grows, they become more responsible and their free time becomes precious. After school, or later college, they will have homework or study time and they will also want to have time with their pals and to start to earn some money for themselves. The opposite sex is becoming important to them and they will start to think what the future could bring at college, university or finding a job.

Parents and teachers confirm to them that good examination results are key to their future and that this is the period of their lives that they should 'knuckle down' to hard work and achieve the grades to place them in college on the next step to finding an occupation to suit them.

Hopefully they will continue with their football as this has undoubtedly given them great joy for a number of years, possibly half of their lives. A good coach will emphasise how well they have done at football, how healthy they are and the great feeling that being fit has done for them in terms of feeling well, few illnesses, feeling mentally sharp, less stressed and being easier to enjoy good sleep. Not forgetting all the friends and great memories that have been enjoyed.

147. A player at this age now has a greater knowledge of his playing position and is aware of his strengths and limitations. They now recognise the importance of winning to themselves and their team-mates. As they grow through the later teens they are becoming more emotionally strong and can cope better with emotions. Their adult personality is now more obvious and they start to understand and see the support that parents, family, friends, teachers and coaches have given them over the years. A player now has a much greater knowledge of general playing positions and they can now evaluate their performance after a match. The skills and repetitions they practised as a younger player are now looking good as their motor ability increases and their main growth spurt period has slowed down. As their bodies fill out and the gangly, leggy look disappears, the body shape is now in better proportions and movements look a lot smoother.

CHAPTER 3

Skill Acquisition

SKILL ACQUISITION

148. Golfers say they are 'in the groove'. In other words, they can visualise themselves taking the club back and striking the ball really well with a previously proven technique. Practising the correct techniques will improve your game immensely, but you must do it for hundreds of hours.

The best players in the world to watch are the flair players who have a great first touch in controlling the ball, and who have the dazzling dribbling skills and imagination to unlock the toughest defences.

This style of professional player costs millions of pounds to buy, yet these players learnt their basic skills either playing street football in South America with their pals or playing beech football in a sunny climate.

There is a saying that 'you can not teach old dogs new tricks' in other words the earlier you teach a youngster skills

57

and tricks the earlier they will master these skills, and with constant repetition they will develop these skills as natural to them as walking is to us.

The current top football managers all agree that with the demise of street football we have seen fewer skilful players coming into the professional game. They are talking about the days when you played 15-a-side in the park with your mates and the match lasted for hours – until your tea was ready, the football burst or you were tired. There was no adult supervision or adult interference telling you what to do and who to pass the ball to.

However, if parents encourage their children to start learning skills, and back this up with regular repetition, star players will again come through.

It is useful to skill acquisition if a player has a good combination of motor abilities such as co-ordination, balance, agility and suppleness.

CONTROLLING THE BALL

149. A player must learn how to control the ball using the four main surfaces of their body, controlling with the foot, thigh, chest and head. The world's best can control and pass the ball with either foot, and control with either the instep, the front of the foot or the outside of the foot. A player must imagine that the ball is an egg and that they are trying to 'cushion' the egg without breaking it.

A parent can develop a nightly fun routine where they throw ten passes to each foot, then ten to each of the chest, thigh and head – although only use very soft foam ball if the youngster is under ten years old. The child can either volley it back to you with their feet, or cushion control onto the floor.

Players need hundreds of hours to develop a feel for the ball but even if the youngster only practises for two hours a week that means he will have achieved over 100 hours of skill practise in two years, which will really make a difference to his skill acquisition. Imagine, though, how good he would be if he practised skills for four hours a week!

DRIBBLING SKILLS

150. A youngster should practise many different ways of skilfully going past an opponent at speed, ensuring that the ball is under control all of the time. They can initially practise by dribbling past a cone or a static object – no, not mum's favourite vase! Once they feel confident, the most effective way of learning is against live moving opposition. Again, the use of both feet is important to unsettle the opponent and make it difficult for them to work out which side you are going to beat them on. Every training session a youngster has at a junior club should include a one-on-one or two-versus-two dribbling session.

PASSING AND CROSSING

151. I love to see a player using reverse or disguised passing. Imagine a right-winger dribbling inside off his wing with the ball and then quickly returning the ball to the wing to his overlapping full-back. That's a reverse pass. A disguised pass is when a player looks one way and passes the ball in a totally different direction. This again puts the opponent off and he then has no idea what the player is going to do next.

A player like David Beckham spent countless hours practising his passing and crossing technique. This ability, once mastered, then became second nature to him and he scored many spectacular free kicks for his clubs and his country by using this quite simple but so effective side footed method.

If youngsters are prepared to practise a correct technique for long hours they too can master the style that has won Beckham and rugby union player Jonny Wilkinson worldwide fame and success.

SHOOTING

152. Obviously, if you score more goals than you let in, you win games. Players of every age love to shoot at the goal and score and with the correct repetition huge improvements can be made in a relatively short time. Most goals from outside of the penalty area are scored with the front of the player's foot. The player's toe is pointing to the ground, and he is trying to make contact with the ball onto his laces. If he can point the laces to the required target area they will gain the required accuracy, especially if their arms are in a position to help balance. If a player is in the penalty area or the six yard area they are likely to score a goal with a side-footed shot or pass, or a header.

SKILFUL THINKING

153. Football practise in a way is likened to golfing practise. A golfer can practise his shot making for many hours but if he is practising using the wrong technique he will never improve and will be a very frustrated player. To improve his golf he will go and have lessons from a golfing professional. Perhaps it would therefore be a good idea to find a well-respected football coach who has a track record in improving football technique. Good practise will bring improvement and enjoyment, however bad practise can bring frustration and a feeling of failure. Practise makes perfect if practised well enough and long enough.

154. Once a skill is nearly mastered and I say nearly, because it must always be practised to keep it sharp, it is stored in the memory and the memory uses the skill in auto pilot fashion when it is needed in the match. Ian Rush the great Liverpool striker was asked how he scored a particular goal and he said that the ball was at his feet and suddenly in a flash it was in the back of the net. He could not recall what his thought process was as he did not have time to work out what to do. It was instinctive and practised over many years with great success. Ian's mind helped him choose the correct technique at the right time. His reactions were razor sharp and his memory (some might say the computer in his head) took over and combined with his technique and his athleticism made scoring goals easy to him. I was nearly involved in a multiple car accident on a motorway in the mid 1990s and to this day I can not explain how I avoided the other vehicles. In a fraction of a second I manoeuvred away from the danger and to a safe place. I feel that my subconscious took over, worked out the options and helped me calmly steer away. There was no way I could have worked out this solution in a split second.

CHAPTER 4

The Coach for Youngsters

WHY BE A FOOTBALL COACH FOR YOUNGSTERS?

'It is a privilege and a great responsibility to be given
the opportunity to coach children and young people.'

155. You probably never considered that you would ever be
a football coach, but you now go and watch your son or
daughter train and play matches and because you are there,
you may as well become involved. Bingo! That's how the
majority of football coaches start.

156. If you have ever watched or played football yourself
you could well think that it's easy and you will make a great
coach with little effort. Well, not exactly. The rewards in
terms of enjoyment could be huge for you and hopefully
for your youngster who is in the squad.

At times you will experience a rollercoaster of emotions

from great highs, when the squad bonds, your players are winning and every team member is happy and their parents are chuffed, to the disappointment when youngsters leave your club because they are not getting enough minutes on the pitch on match day, the team can't win a match and confidence is low.

A good coach is always learning and has an open mind. A positive coach will learn from other coaches and from other sports and will take on modern coaching ideas and techniques. A good coach will share his ideas with others and will go out of his way to support and mentor new coaches.

CREATING A POSITIVE ENVIRONMENT

'Enjoyment is one central principle of my
managerial approach, I am massive on enjoyment.'
SIR CLIVE WOODWARD, COACH OF THE 2003 WORLD CUP
WINNING ENGLAND RUGBY UNION TEAM

157. As Kevin Costner said in the great movie *Field of Dreams*, 'Build it and they will come'. That was my objective when I started my football academy in 1997, and within two weeks we had 240 players. If you can provide a coaching setup where the players are comfortable and content, then you have a good foundation to build upon.

158. The atmosphere that you decide to create is key to the success and enjoyment of the players, fellow coaches and parents. If a parent sees their child having fun, learning new skills, building new friendships and wanting to come to training at every opportunity then you are on the road to creating the correct atmosphere. Once word gets around that you have a happy environment then more youngsters will want to join you.

159. Setting the scene from the outset is very important and I believe that it is good to show players and parents that your attitude is geared towards enjoyment at all times, as is the fact that you do not have a 'win at all costs' mentality. While you should stress that fun is top of your agenda when coaching children, you should equally state there is a code of conduct and discipline that everybody must adhere to. The simple objective of this discipline is to ensure that everybody's enjoyment is maximised and that one person doesn't spoil things for the others. After your first training session you can hand out copies of your code of conduct – one for the players and one for the parents. Once they have read it you can ask them to sign it to say that they will adhere to the rules. Parents will welcome this and will be impressed with your organisation.

160. The atmosphere will be happy, and the players will not be afraid of making a mistake. The parents will see that you are looking at what the players are good at and not always criticising them for what they are not so good at.

THE COACH'S ATTITUDE

'Love what you do, enthusiasm is infectious, and your
energy and commitment will rub off on others.'

SIR BOBBY ROBSON

161. Everybody loves to spend time in the company of
people with a positive attitude. Youngsters will think that
their coach is great if you can always give them a welcoming,
enthusiastic greeting when you see them. Always call them
by their first name. A fun atmosphere can be further created
if a player has a nickname that he is happy to be called by. It
is good to be pleasant with the parents but there is no
requirement to make them your best mates.

162. If you give the players 99% praise they will enjoy
being involved in your group or team and they will work
even harder to keep improving and to receive further praise
from you.

163. A good sense of humour is so important to children
in particular and having a laugh with the coach once again
enhances the relationship and makes the youngsters
comfortable. This can be further improved when the coach
finds out the interests of the player, which he will then use
when motivating them. A coach should respect whichever
team their youngsters support and not make fun of them,
even in a joking way.

164. An enthusiastic coach is popular, especially if they show excitement when a player achieves a new skill, or makes or scores a goal. This will motivate the players to mirror the coach's enthusiasm and excitement level.

In life it's the way we react to situations, both good and bad, that determines our happiness or sadness. If we choose to find positives, even out of negative situations, we will develop the confidence to deal with most situations that arise.

A bad coach is one who tries to give players things they are incapable of doing and who pushes them even if they don't want to do something. When you can't get the maximum from your players you need to perhaps change your style of talking to them. Are you too serious when they simply want to enjoy themselves? Or maybe they need more freedom to express themselves – are you suppressing this freedom?

165. Consider your attitude as a coach at the moment. Do you see the world in a happy way or do you just see problems across the globe and in your personal life? For the next two weeks, have the determination and focus to wake up in the morning and see everything in a positive light.

If you can then make this away of life and turn it into a habit then the difference in your life will be amazing. You could be taking life far too seriously – perhaps you need to lighten up and try to enjoy every minute of every day. This new relaxed and positive you will attract people to you and you will feel much more happier. The players you coach and their parents will certainly be pleased to see a happy you.

166. You might wonder why your players play well in training, but not in matches. The simple answer is pressure. In training they are more relaxed, they have no fear of making mistakes and they enjoy themselves. A good coach will encourage them to enjoy their football in matches, to work hard of course, but a good coach will actually give their players permission to make mistakes. There is, however, a good form of pressure which motivates youngsters to enjoy their football and creates an excitement which drives them forward to win games.

167. A children's coach needs to be liked by the players and their parents. This is not to say that the parents and coach must become great mates. As you are the one coaching and selecting the team you have to be seen to be totally 100% unbiased. If you are seen to be friendlier with one parent than another, and you leave out other players from the team, you will be accused of being biased. Friendships have been put under strain and have ended when you have had to leave out a player whose parents you have befriended. 'A thoughtful person is a remembered person'.

168. The coach must encourage all the players and make sure that they all receive the same attention from him. A good coach will look to improve the player's individual skills and teamwork and will be more focused on improving the performance rather than concentrating on the result of the match. A positive coach will understand that children must be treated totally differently from adults and that each player and each age group has different characteristics.

169. If all your players train and play matches with enthusiasm, energy and a determination to do well, you are succeeding. If at the end of training and matches they are happy and content with their effort and they have smiles on their faces, you as the coach are winning. Notice I have not mentioned whether the team won or lost. In children's football the key is enjoyment. Full stop!

THE THINKING COACH

'A good coach paints pictures, the simpler the better.'
RON GREENWOOD, FORMER WEST HAM
AND ENGLAND MANAGER

170. The thinking coach will look smart at all times and set the correct example. His kit, football boots and trainers will be clean and modern and his appearance will be clean and fresh.

171. He will be organised and his session plan will be prepared well in advance, taking into consideration the age, ability and physical strengths of his players. It is a good idea for a coach to keep all his session plans in a file for him to use at a later date. Make a note after each session plan, commenting on how the session was received by the players, what they particularly enjoyed, whether the session was fully suitable to their age and ability, and how the session could be improved. Then give the session a mark out of ten.

172. A forward-thinking coach will set objectives for the players to achieve. The objectives for the children will be very basic, such as improving a shooting technique within a given time, or doing so many keep-ups, or learning two different turns with the ball. The coach will really want the players to achieve the objective and will reward them with generous praise. Older players can be asked to improve their fitness, or make three accurate passes in a row, or play so many one-twos in training or in matches, or perhaps improve on their disguised passing.

It is correct to put in a sensible time frame to achieve their goals, and these objectives need to be agreed with the players. They must be testing but achievable.

There will be different levels of ability within the team so it is correct to give each player tasks at their own level. If a task is too hard the player will know this and will struggle, which could de-motivate him and lower his confidence. Make all tasks realistically achievable and have short-, mid- and long-term objectives both for individual players and the team.

173. The equipment a good coach uses will be modern and appropriate to the age of the players. The footballs will be the correct size and will be inflated to the correct pressure. The training bibs will be the correct size, they will be clean and there will be a good mix of colour options.

174. The training session will set realistic objectives, making sure that is not too easy (which would lead to boredom) and not too difficult (which may de-motivate the players). There are many good coaching books available to purchase, from books about coaching very young players to in-depth books for elite players in their teens. Contact your local or county football association and they will supply you with suggestions. Keep football simple.

175. Before the players arrive, the training equipment should be set up and the training areas and pitches should be coned off as required. The training session should start at the agreed time and place. This is a good habit to get into and it will set the tone of your disciplinary requirements. If players are late on a regular basis, ask their parents if they can arrive on time as it disrupts the session.

176. The coach will be aware of the type of session that his players enjoy the most and he will plan accordingly to satisfy their needs, making sure that there is a good variation of football activities to maintain their interest and motivation. As a guide all children, youths and adults love shooting sessions and one-on-one dribbling sessions. If you have, say, six variations of shooting sessions you can call upon, plus six dribbling or one-on-one sessions, and you introduce some of them at most training sessions, your players will go home happy, providing that you end each session with small-sided competitive matches. Use about a third of the full session for this.

177. It is important that players understand the words and descriptions that the coach uses, and it is vital that he combines words with a demonstration of the task that he is asking the players to perform. 'Well played' or 'great shot' are positive comments for a task achieved; however you should sometimes try to be more specific in your comments, such as 'Great shot, John – your style and technique were good and you looked at the goalkeeper's position before shooting'. Look for the things your players are good at and don't keep mentioning the things they are not so good at.

178. Each coaching session could well involve a fun warm-up, or a tag game, which will immediately put the players in good spirits. Once the muscles are warm, stretching can take place followed by a skills session where players can have a lot of touches of the ball and can practise and hopefully, with repetition, master their chosen skill. A shooting session or a one-on-one dribbling session could be next, followed by small-sided matches to finish. End this session with stretches again and a few minutes' debrief where plenty of praise is given. Make sure you have plenty of footballs so that the session is not stop-start while you are waiting for footballs to be returned. Happy players will then look forward to the next training session or match.

179. The thinking coach will continually look to improve his knowledge and will be open to new ideas and coaching methods. The open-minded coach will learn from others and will watch and copy how other coaches interact with their players. This coach will go on development courses and will purchase the recommended coaching books and DVDs. They will also improve their knowledge of sports science, nutrition and first aid. Once they have achieved a coaching grade they will look to see what work is required to move to the next level.

180. The thinking coach will be a good listener and will learn from coaches and managers at all levels. He will also watch matches involving children, youngsters and adults at local, semi and full professional and International levels. It is fascinating to watch how the top managers act, compared to the managers at the lower end of the league. Watch the top guys on TV. They generally sit and chew their gum, looking relatively relaxed, but with an element of match anxiety. They know that their players are at the top of their profession and that they have experienced most situations in the best and most hostile stadiums in the world. There is not a lot the manager can do now as his players kick off. He trusts them and he sits back and tries to enjoy the match.

Watch the manager at the bottom end of the same league. His team are threatened with possible relegation and his job is on the line. His players are on a losing streak and their confidence is somewhat lacking. He will be on the touchline for most of the game, encouraging, cajoling and driving his players to put in great effort. He will be looking to influence the match officials to give his team every close decision and he will be hoping that his enthusiastic and animated actions will drive his players on.

181. A good coach who wants the respect of his players will not shout at them, but will ensure that all the players understand him. It could well be that the coach is at fault and he has not explained his requirements well enough. If the coach makes an error it is good that he is honest enough to admit it and the players will then copy this when they have made a mistake instead of blaming others. Professional players switch off and lose respect for coaches who are always shouting at them and who criticise them in the media. The top coaches have the respect of their players who know that any criticism from the coach will be made to them privately and not in the glare of the media.

182. The coach will understand that all children are uniquely different and that they learn in different ways and at different speeds. He will get to know each youngster's strengths and weaknesses, and in conversation with them, he will find out what they enjoy about football. He will then tailor-make his sessions using their motivations and interests.

183. As we know, confidence is king and the thinking coach will work to really boost the players' confidence and self esteem by giving them constant praise and catching them doing good things so that he can reward them with further praise.

184. There are negative coaches out there who will focus on what the player can't do rather than looking for the very good things that the player can do. A coach who moans all the time has a negative effect on the players – not only can they come to dislike the coach but their own confidence can be severely dented. This style of coach will never bring out the very best in his players.

185. When you need to correct a fault, tell the team or individual that you are pleased with their overall performance and that you would like them to give some focus to areas where they can show further improvement. This subtle way of asking them to improve on a mistake is done in a positive rather than a negative way and should, with focus, cure the problem.

This is well known in football as the 'praise sandwich'. For example, you could say to a player that he is playing really well, but that to improve his game even further he could look up that little bit earlier and see the striker making an early run. Finish by saying that you are very pleased with his overall game. This way you are not ruining the player's confidence, but praising him as well as providing him with an important tip.

186. Positive coaches know that effort, combined with confidence, are the very basic ingredients that players can build upon. A positive coach understands that lazy skills showing little effort or passion will not be effective. There are players in every team who are not as gifted as others in terms of ball skills; however these players often give everything to the team and their effort should be highlighted by the coach. Skill without effort does not work, but you can get away with less skill as long as you're putting the effort in.

187. A thinking coach will know that each player's skills are vital, but only when combined with a great team effort where every player works hard to win the ball back quickly when possession has been lost. Then, as a team, they can break forward at speed using skill and accurate passing to deliver an attempt at goal.

188. As a young player at Manchester United I was continually encouraged to enjoy my football and play without fear of making a mistake. The words 'Football is a simple game; let the ball do the work' were used on a daily basis and 'Do the simple things very well' was regularly mentioned. 'Simplicity is genius' were words that we were continually bombarded with. Many junior team managers get involved with complicated tactics that they hardly understand themselves, never mind their young players. The best managers on the planet buy the best players available to them and put them into a team shape. They then trust them to perform.

When I see managers changing formation during a match from 4-2-4 to 4-5-1 and then to 4-4-2 I laugh as they are trying to be too clever. In most cases the players do not understand and are not happy with the changes. Keep it simple – that's what all the best managers in history have done.

189. The coach will need to be patient as he knows that it will take many years of practise and repetition to master the skill required. There are many skills in football, not just the ones used by the gifted dribblers and creative players. An aggressively-timed tackle is a great skill and will again be the result of many hours of honed practise. When you see gifted professional sportspeople perform, thousands of hours have been taken up in practising the desired skill.

190. A classic saying in life is 'learn from your mistakes'. A coach to youngsters must allow the players to make mistakes and then show them how to correct the error. If the coach speaks to his player in a calm way, they will improve the mistake in a learning way. If the player is shouted at he will not try a particular skill again as he faces being criticised again and will feel that he is under pressure.

191. A thoughtful coach will know that youngsters can sometimes improve really quickly, but then stop this improvement – and even go backwards – before improving again. As each youngster is different, there can be many reasons for this, including body changes, confidence or motivational change and perhaps family issues or things happening at school. Perseverance and patience is required by the coach and the player and if they continue to work together the player can soon start to move upwards and forwards again.

192. The safety of the youngsters is obviously the number one priority. The training or match surface should always be checked before training commences to make sure it is safe and the goals must be 100% safe before using them. If you have any doubt about the goals, DO NOT USE THEM and report the fault to the owner of the goals before anybody else uses them. A number of youngsters are badly injured and even killed every year by unsafe goals collapsing on them. Parents can play a part by making sure the coach has checked the goal safety by doing so themselves. Keep checking during the game, as a strong shot or heavy wind could dislodge the goal structure.

193. At every training session or match, take your emergency first aid bag with you to treat minor injuries. I have a database of all my players' names, addresses and parents' home and mobile telephone numbers. I always have a copy with me in case I need to contact a parent in an emergency. My mobile telephone is with me at all times in case I need to make important calls. Thankfully, I have rarely had to call a parent to collect a poorly or injured player. Is it pure luck that in a contact sport such as football we have had few injuries? Possibly yes, but we work hard and think well to minimise potential injury risks.

Put together an injury book and log any injuries that occur, when and how the incident happened, what the injury was and how you dealt with it.

194. Everybody involved with the club including the manager, coach, Secretary and Treasurer should be first aid trained and hold the appropriate certificate. You should become really knowledgeable in first aid because not only will it help you on the football pitch, but one day you might even save someone's life.

195. Parents and you as the coach are very influential in a young person's life. One thing I regard as a very important part of coaching is teaching players to have respect for their team-mates, the opposition and the match officials. I applaud my players when they praise a team-mate for a good pass or a goal-saving tackle, but if I saw a youngster criticising the referee or another match official I would substitute him immediately. I would then remind him that his actions were unacceptable and remind him of the club code of conduct which he would have received at the beginning of the season.

196. I am immensely proud of my youngsters at my Masterskills Football Academy, where we have 300 players aged from five to 15 years old. In our training sessions I tell them individually how well they are doing and in regular newsletters I thank the players for their enthusiasm and hard work and I thank their parents for allowing them to come to my Academy. It is important to create a good feeling where everybody appreciates each other's commitment.

197. Don't be a stop-start coach. What I mean by this is to let your training sessions flow. Don't keep stopping the session to correct every fault so that everybody gets cold and bored. Make notes and at drink breaks and after the session make short comments of less than two minutes in total. The kids will not be able to take in many corrections in one go and it is always good to finish a session on a fun, high note if possible so that they will enthusiastically come back for more.

198. As you complete the training session ask the players to collect in all the cones, bibs and footballs and only give them 60 seconds to do it. Give some players a job to do each session or every week for a month and then rotate them. For early arrivers it could be helping you take the equipment from your car to the pitch and helping you set the markers and cones out for the training session. Or when you select the teams in matches, a player could be responsible for making sure everyone has the correct colour bib. They love to help the coach and by giving them a time limit provides a competitive edge. It makes them feel a more important member of the team and they feel a commitment to the club.

199. As each session ends, we complete our stretches and then I award a sticker to three players for good performance. The winners of stickers might have scored the best goal or worked hardest on the pitch, or they could have shown a great skill, good sportsmanship or just a great attitude. The stickers focus their minds on positive performance, good concentration and good behaviour.

200. Young children need to play in weather conditions that are comfortable to them and are not too cold or not too hot. They do not mind playing on a muddy pitch but playing in rain is unsuitable for them and you want to encourage them to continue with their football. It is okay to play in cold conditions provided as long as the players are wearing warm clothing, including tracksuit bottoms, woolly hats and gloves. If it's icy cold and the pitch is unsuitable try to use an indoor facility where the youngsters can still practise their skills and play five-a-side matches. 'Embrace and enjoy every training session'.

COACH COMMUNICATION

'Always look for the best in people, respect them and watch for opportunities to praise them.'

201. It is important that what you say and how you say it is interpreted in a positive way by your players. Your facial expression and body language are also important to the players and their families. Stand tall, look at your audience and select your words so that everybody fully understands you. Communication is not always *what* you say but *how* you say it. If you are giving players instruction and they look away from you, there is a good chance that they do not understand you. A smiling, contented coach will bring the same reaction from the players.

202. When a new youngster joins your group, go over the top with praise and tell them you are really pleased that they have joined. They will be uncertain at first, especially if they do not know any of the other players. Encourage your players to call the newcomer by their first name and look to praise at every opportunity. Ask a couple of your players to look after the new player and ask them to also praise him when he achieves a success. Do not criticise or make any negative comments, and the player will feel totally integrated with the group within a few weeks.

203. Children and youngsters are comfortable with a smiling coach who not only compliments them, but who can instil common sense and discipline when needed without shouting. A good coach has the desire to help others and the youngsters will soon sense this and want to play for this coach. A coach that persuades a player to try or do something instead of telling him to do something will have soon gained the respect of the player.

204. Positive body language is important. If your body is slumped with your head and shoulders down and your arms flaying, even the younger children will detect your displeasure with them. Body language is powerful so do not underestimate its effectiveness, both in a positive way and a negative way. Make sure you are aware of your body language at all times and that it is always positive.

205. Your voice should be versatile. Shouting at children is a no-go! Keep everything bouncing along and keep changing the pitch of your voice. Keep it enthusiastic at all times. Your players will enjoy listening to you, especially when you deliver your comments on the good things from the training session or the match. If a player is not behaving well tell them that you want them to continue training with you but only if their behaviour is good. If the poor behaviour or lack of attention continues you might need to have a word with the youngster's parents.

206. In life, genuine self-criticism is appreciated and people warm to you if you knock yourself occasionally. I laugh with our very young players and parents and tell them that I am better at tying bootlaces than I am as a coach, as I've had so much practise! Nobody likes a big-headed coach who has a know-it-all attitude, but people warm to coaches who are organised and have a professional attitude with a caring personality.

207. History in football has proved that good communicators have enjoyed success. Whether the players are five years old or experienced professionals they all appreciate a common-sense coach who is constantly positive and well organised, who can instil discipline and who can have a laugh with his players, win or lose.

208. Encourage feedback from your players. Ask them what they most enjoy about training and playing matches, and also what they do not like or enjoy. Remember that it is their game, so you can take their comments on board and adapt your training sessions to maximise their enjoyment. The three things they are likely to say is that they love to play matches in training, they love a variety of shooting sessions and one-on-one dribbling sessions. I like to give them plenty of time with a ball each in training, to practise their skills in a range of fun competitive activities. They are actually doing a lot of running with the ball but they do not realise it as they are enjoying skill time. This is actually a good ploy if you want to do a running session as they will run longer and happier if they have a ball at their feet.

209. If you sense the players have had a bad day on the training pitch, or if they've suffered a heavy defeat, then discuss it and put the smile back on their faces. Put on a fun training session that you know they will really enjoy. It will focus their minds and it is a great way to release tension and anxiety. Many professional managers actually give targeted criticism after a win rather than a defeat. A player will find it easier to take on a constructive point after a win than after a defeat. It also makes sure that the players keep their feet on the ground and do not get complacent.

210. Whatever you say do not reduce the players confidence or self esteem. Confidence and self esteem can take a long time to build, but can take seconds to destroy. If you show players up in front of their team-mates they will grow to dislike you and not trust you anymore. They can feel betrayed.

211.

Good coach	Bad coach
Very positive attitude	Negative attitude
Always organised	Disorganised
Good planner	Does not plan ahead
Very enthusiastic	Little enthusiasm
Wants to learn and improve	Thinks he knows everything
Looks at improving performance	Win-only mentality
Encourages all the time	Criticises all mistakes
Gives praise	Shouts at players
Good relationship with parents	Does not speak to parents

In professional football successful coaches do not really believe in luck but have a great desire to win and achieve their ambitions.

DEALING WITH PROBLEMS

212. Some positive people will say, 'There are no such things as problems, just challenges'. That s a very positive way to look at things. Always take into consideration the other persons point of view before you make a verbal comment. If you see the problem through their eyes, the solution can usually be solved in a prompt and mutually satisfactory way. Hopefully the other person also wants to solve the problem. If a problem is mutually resolved, relationships can actually be strengthened.

213. Some people will brush problems under the carpet and hope they will go away while others will deal with a problem head-on. The problem–solvers will find out the reason and cause of the problem and will communicate with people to try and resolve the problem without anyone's feelings being hurt. A good listener is important, and if people see that you care about them they will try and help come to a solution.

How you deal with issues that occur is as important as how you coach the youngsters. Sometimes a coach or manager will be judged more on how he deals with problems and difficult situations than how he acts in good situations. Whatever problems occur, it is important that you as the leader remain cool and considered under pressure. Sometimes it is better to say to somebody that you would just like a short period to think over the issue before you get back to them. This can mean that both parties can 'cool down' and then think through a sensible solution. We have all wished we had reacted better to a situation and perhaps been a little more diplomatic, but hopefully we can learn from our past experiences.

214. As a coach of youngsters the biggest issue you will have to deal with is unhappy or unruly parents. Don't worry – 98% of them are great and the occasionally overenthusiastic ones just get carried away with the excitement of the game. The main issues arise when parents believe that their youngster is not getting enough playing time on the pitch, either because they are starting as a substitute or not getting on the pitch at all. In children's football it is up to you to select the matchday squad and ensure that all the players have good playing time. Don't have too many substitutes if you don't believe that you will be able to give them all a decent length of match time, especially when they have travelled many miles to an away match. It is much better to split the players into two teams and play against two teams that the opposition has also put together. Players want to play, as the only thing they learn standing on a cold touchline is that they don't want to stand there again.

215. Make sure that you have a football coaching qualification or that you are working towards one. You have to look the part and your coaching must be structured and be effective. You do not want parents questioning your ability to coach their children, believing they could do better. This little bit of pressure is a good motivation for you to gain further coaching awards and first aid practical experience.

216. You have to ensure that everybody enjoys the matchday experience and you share this responsibility with your opposing coach and manager. You should also want the match official to enjoy their game, because that's what they are in it for. As you will have given the parents a code of conduct, they should know their responsibilities. However, emotions and passions can run high during a match and they may need reminding of these responsibilities – especially if the opposing team's management and parents are poorly behaved. Keep a cool head and quietly remind individuals that you would like them to calm down as you want all the children to enjoy themselves.

When emotions have calmed down after the game, you might want to have a discreet word with the troublemakers, or you might want to leave it until the following day when you can either call them or send them a letter outlining what their poor behaviour could potentially have led to. Repeating their bad actions is no good for anybody and if you do not deal with it immediately your strength of personality and character will be questioned. If the behaviour continues, you have little alternative but to ask the parent not to come to watch matches or even to ask them not to bring their child to training – which should of course be the last resort.

217. If you make your coaching sessions attractive to the children, so that they can't wait to come to the next session, then you will have gone a long way towards lowering the risk of potential problems. Parents will not want their children to miss out on something they clearly enjoy doing, and they will hopefully therefore try to control their behaviour at matches.

218. If parents have a problem with the coach, they can either discuss it with the coach directly or call the club secretary or welfare officer. A children's coach should have the right attitude and should be approachable at all times. If your relationship with the parents is friendly, conflicts should rarely occur. In conversations with parents, other players should never be criticised. Coaches and parents should try to defuse any problems and work towards solving them. Coaches should not make promises they can't keep, such as saying they will give certain players more match time and then not keeping that promise.

219. A former manager of mine, Tom Johnson at Huddersfield Town, used to say 'Don't lose a goal and you won't lose a game, and if they don't score a goal and we score one we win'. How simply but so clearly put. Tom Johnson left the club only 10 days after I joined, which was a disappointment as I would have loved to have heard more of his legendary team talks.

I had an interesting first meeting with Tom Johnson. I signed my contract with Huddersfield Town only one hour before a home match, nothing surprising there, but with 20 minutes to kick-off I was still in his office sharing my second cup of tea and biscuits with him as he sat in his slippers with his dog at his feet. In a very relaxed state of mind, he invited me to join him in the stand as the players kicked off.

I recall one of Tom's matches, when he was a couple of minutes late in leaving the dressing room. As he strode down the tunnel, one of his players was coming towards him in an agitated state. 'Son, don't you think you had better be getting on the pitch ready for kick-off?' Tom said firmly. 'Go away, Gaffer,' replied the player, 'I've just been sent off'. One of football's quickest ever sendings-off and the manager hadn't even reached the dugout to see it!

Tom had his own way of solving problems in a very relaxed manner but with some dry humour he certainly got his message across. Huddersfield Town were in the lower divisions and had come upon hard financial times. The club's history was very good, though, reaching and winning a number of FA Cup finals in its earlier years.

'The optimist turns problems into opportunities and the pessimist turns opportunities into problems.'

220. At Manchester United Tommy Docherty was known as a great motivator with a cutting sense of humour. His first team coach, Tom Cavanagh, warned all the players that the Doc could be your best friend or your worst enemy. He believed in all of the players giving their all at all times. He had this fantastic ability to make you feel ten feet tall, but he would not stand for indiscipline. Our highly respected captain Martin Buchan once disagreed with the Boss on the training field and was quickly sent packing to the changing rooms. Nobody dared cross the Doc. He dealt with problems quite clearly. If he didn't agree with you, you were not in his favour, but thanks to the Doc I also witnessed the best piece of motivation I ever seen. He purchased a well-known striker for a lot of money but the player struggled in a team that was low in confidence. High passes were continually punted forward to this diminutive forward, who had little chance converting them. The forward became injured, and the boss became unsure of the players commitment to the team's cause. One lunchtime after training all the professional players, from the full internationals to the young pros, were summand to meet in the first-team dressing room at the Cliff training ground. Nobody had any idea what was to come but if it was meant to shock us all it certainly had the desired effect. All the players were changed into our clothes except the striker, who was in a dressing gown after coming from the treatment table.

Tommy Docherty verbally launched into an aggressive stance against the injured player, calling him the worst player he had ever purchased, a waste of money and calling him a disgrace to Manchester United. This onslaught lasted for five minutes before the player was told to get back to his treatment table. As the Doc left, 44 professional players sat in stunned silence before making our way home. The player was normally a great professional but was frustrated at not being given great service by his team-mates to score the goals the team badly needed. His confidence was at a low and the boss believed he was faking injury.

Did the player sulk and leave the club? No. Did the manager kick him out of the club? No. He wanted to prove the Doc wrong and he certainly did. The player returned to the first team, and would you believe it, the boss put him forward as the player of the season. The manager knew what would motivate this particular player and this player went on to become a fans' favourite at Old Trafford, winning many more international caps for his country. Tommy Docherty had his own unique style of dealing with problems and on this occasion it worked wonders.

Not all players in a team get along and the same goes for parents. It is part of normal life; however it is in everybody's interests that everybody understands that the game is 100% based on the children's enjoyment. Sometimes the only solution can be a player moving clubs to find enjoyment.

I like this quote from a professional football manager: 'The worst thing about being a football manager is keeping the six players who hate you away from the five players who are undecided.'

CHAPTER 5

Footballing Parents

PARENT AND CHILD FOOTBALL RELATIONSHIP

221. Generally speaking, parents love their child with a tremendous passion and great pride. They can give their youngster bags of praise, but as experienced coaches will confirm, some parents in football can cause big problems.

222. Make time for your child. They want to see Mum and Dad more than they want to see the pay they bring home. Parents who play with their children and play an active part in their lives provide those children with a happy life. Studies show that these children move on to have more success and are more socially confident. The children who were brought up predominantly by their mother did little better than the children brought up in single-parent families. Although fathers tend to spend more time with their sons, both sexes enjoy interaction with their dads.

223. It is one of my major rules that parents do not shout out instruction to their youngsters at training, and certainly not during matches. Imagine yourself as a child on a football pitch, and then imagine that four people are giving you different instructions all at the same time for the duration of the match, while the ball is whizzing around at speed. Not easy! At almost every junior match I attend, I see adults and parents bawling out instructions that quite simply are too difficult for the kids to understand and action.

The basic need for your child is to enjoy his football with a freedom to experiment. The only adult instruction should be from the coach and this should be kept to a minimum. I do believe, however, that it is great to cheer and shout 'well done' and show enthusiasm.

224. Parents and other adults can quickly destroy the confidence that they and the coach have worked so hard to build up. Kids are playing for their own enjoyment, not for their parents' enjoyment. Allow them to enjoy their football, win, draw or lose, and you as adults will be thrilled to see them happy and contented.

Tell your children how great, beautiful or handsome they are and never be afraid to put your arms around them and give them a hug. My son and daughter, Michael and Helen, are in their mid-twenties and they always receive regular hugs. That will continue until I am six feet under.

225. When the coaching session or match is over, parents should immediately give their children the thumbs-up with enthusiastic praise, and applaud the efforts of the whole team and the opponents. I used to love it when my eight-year-old son and I discussed his forthcoming matches as we sat on the sofa and enthusiastically watched *Match of the Day* on a Saturday evening.

226. We all naturally like to win and winning provides a real feel-good factor. Children sometimes do find defeat difficult to accept. It is up to the coach and parents to stress that both winning and losing are acceptable parts of life and that you were so pleased with the great effort they gave.

227. I love to see parents focus on the good things that their children do rather than stressing the things that they are not so good at. Remember, 'confidence is king' and seeing their own children excel in what they do fills parents with great joy. It is a good thing to praise other children too, especially when things have not gone to plan and somebody needs a boost. If your children see the compassion you show to others they will copy this great strength you have. If you give other children praise I am sure their parents will reciprocate and praise your youngster.

228. Good performance stickers go down well as does a 'Player of the Month' certificate or trophy. At our annual presentation evening, all our players receive a trophy and a certificate and for each age group, 12 major trophies are awarded. This type of award is a nice bonus for the children but ongoing praise is the biggest confidence booster, especially from the coach, fellow players and parents.

229. You are a role model to your child and in every situation they will watch to see how you conduct yourself. They will copy how you greet people, smile, laugh and interact with people and sometimes they can pick up habits that you are not happy with yourself. So be aware of the huge influence you have as a parent. Your kids will copy how you look, and your attitude and your enthusiasm will be mirrored. The influence you have on your children is very powerful, so use it well.

230. Do parents project their own unfulfilled childhood hopes through their children? In some cases, yes, but generally I believe that loud touchline parents just don't get it. They don't understand that it's not *their* match, it's their children's match and their children's time for enjoyment. Do not show your child up with your poor behaviour.

231. As a coach it's important that if you see any behaviour from a parent that you do not agree with, you approach that parent in a non-aggressive manner and explain that their behaviour and attitude is spoiling the experience for everyone and that you as the coach are responsible for everybody's welfare. If a parent on the opposing team is causing a problem, it is a good idea for you as the coach to ask the opposition coach to help solve the problem.

232. The most important people on a football pitch, after the players, are the referee and match officials. They do a fantastic job and obviously without them games would not take place. They have the most difficult job in football as they can't make everybody happy. There are so many things going on during a match and the referee is expected to see everything and get it right every time. It is simply an impossible task. The football 'experts' on TV don't help as they continually criticise referees for mistakes when they have luxury of sitting in a studio with freeze-frame playbacks and slow-motion replays. Add to this the fact that most matches in junior football don't even have assistant referees to judge offsides and throw-ins.

Referees have to give a split-second decision with up to 22 players moving around at speed with some players trying to cheat to gain a free kick or a penalty.

I would recommend that as part of a coach's education they are given a match to referee with no assistant referees. I would also say to parents who have the bad habit of questioning decisions that they should come and referee a training match. They need to take into account, though, that taking charge of a small sided game of seven-a-side with no offsides is much easier than officiating in a match of 11v11 with offsides and 22 players on the pitch, especially when it is a local derby and teams are competing to win the league or avoid relegation.

I can assure them that they will see football in a different light and they will perhaps understand the difficulty that match officials face in getting decisions right. And they might even enjoy the experience and want to take the course to become a match official.

233. Not everybody can openly come forward and tell the world of their enduring love for their parents but it is refreshing to see somebody do it.

I am sure you love your children and parents with passion, so there is no better time than now to tell them so and then keep telling them on a regular basis.

Time spent with your young children could be the most enjoyable years of your lives. Do not miss this opportunity as the days, weeks, months and years can fly by and suddenly your babies are teenagers and ready to leave home for university or work away from home. Take lots of photos and video recordings of your child and youngster at every stage. Seeing video footage of you and your children ten years ago can be hilariously funny. As the Monty Python song says, 'always look on the bright side of life'.

CHAPTER 6

Football Mentality

'There is no such thing as a great talent without
great willpower.'

HONORE DE BALZAC 1789–1850

POSITIVE ATTITUDE

234. Our attitude is affected by our personality and people
that surround us have an important part to play. As a child,
our parents have a major role in our development and
influence, and as we develop into a teenager our peers start
to take over from the parental influence. Role models can
affect the attitude of the individual and it is important that
a young person is surrounded by positive people with a
genuine caring nature. A person who is motivated, and
who has a good attitude and a happy personality will attract
other positive people and this combination, together with
hard work, can achieve success. Hard-working people are
seen to have a positive attitude, and hard working players

on a professional football team are loved by their fellow players and fans alike. Supporters will put up with players who are a little short on ability, if they give their all on the pitch. This style of player usually ends up as the captain of the team.

'Our lives are not determined by what happens to us, but how we react to what happens, not what life brings to us, but by the attitude we bring to life. A positive attitude causes a chain reaction of positive thoughts, events and outcomes. It is a catalyst...a spark that brings extraordinary results.'

AUTHOR UNKNOWN

CONFIDENCE AND SELF ESTEEM

'Ensure your players dream of success and not fear failure'

235. Confidence, attitude and effort are the three most important mental needs of a winning footballer. If a player has a weakness in any of these areas they will not function at their best. If their confidence is high, they have a positive attitude to compete and they give their maximum effort they will enjoy many positive moments in football.

236. We can all recall those moments when we felt really confident. There are certain events that can trigger a boost in confidence. In football it can be a great shot or a piece of skill, a great pass, a crunching tackle to stop a marauding forward or a diving save to stop a certain goal. In your mind, build up a history of positive events that you can recall to confirm how good you are. Golfer Gary Player put it perfectly when he said 'Memories are the cushions of life.' In his experience he has enjoyed fantastic success over five decades and he has stored these achievements in his mind to visualise and recall when he needs a boost to his confidence.

237. Keep telling yourself how good you are. There is a saying that goes 'If you do not tell yourself how good you are nobody else will'. Actively and mentally feel good about yourself. A great base for confidence is being fit. If you combine hard work and regular skill repetition, your confidence will be high and you will have a feeling that almost anything is possible. Just simply say to yourself 'I can do that', smile and recall all your great football moments.

238. Self esteem is a measurement of how we feel about ourselves in our everyday lives. We are conscious of our looks and our appearance, we compare ourselves with others and we imagine what is must be like to live the life of an attractive world famous actor/actress or pop star. At times we look at different ways to motivate and feel good about ourselves. Top footballers have the strength of high self esteem and lower division players have a lower self esteem. The best players have a confidence, and they know they are good players where the lower division players are unsure about themselves, and are a little unpredictable and take less risks. If they make an error their confidence can quickly deflate or if they do something really well they can be on a high again. Their emotions are all over the place, suffering a rollercoaster effect. A good understanding coach can really help this type of player, and the coach will be rewarded with a much improved performer.

239. When you see a sporting legend perform at their very best you see how easy it is for them and you wonder at their natural talent. You are seeing only a snippet of their lives and you are not seeing the many hundreds of thousand of practise shots they have taken. We have not seen the hours that Cristiano Ronaldo and Lionel Messi have put in the garden, yard or park when they were youngsters to master their collections of wonderful skills and techniques. The more you practise the more confidence you build and this confidence gives you a surge of motivation to practise more. This is part in the chain of success.

240. Positive people are great to be involved with. Their positive attitude will influence you and your confidence will grow. Surround yourself with positive people and try to avoid those people who are negative and drain your energy. High achievers exude confidence and they display good body language, while doubters are hunched and talk about the bad weather, the poor economy and everything in negative terms.

241. Confident footballers display happy, confident body language, they are well organised, they know what it takes to ensure their bodies are fit, and they have the mental strength to enjoy success. Confident players play with a free mind, and they are not afraid to make mistakes. They feel less pressure, they take more risks on the field than other players and they want the ball all of the time. These players are regulars in the team and they have built up their confidence knowing that they have earned their place in the team through good consistent performances. A number of professional managers like to rotate players even though the players do not agree with his strategy. Players build up a confidence playing regular consecutive matches. A stop-start philosophy actually interrupts the flow of their confidence and does more harm than good. When a player is in a confidence stride they want to play in every match. When a player is playing well he is not tired and he wants to play in every game. Winning matches energises players whereas losing matches saps their energy.

242. Less confident players tend to be quieter and to play safe football as they are more afraid of making mistakes and possibly receiving criticism. Their body language is more hunched, with their heads down, and they avoid eye contact. Both confident and less confident players can improve greatly if they receive praise and reward in front of their team-mates. Their coach and manager must openly tell them how much they are valued by the team and the coaches. A player who is given constant praise in front of his peers will love his coach and will run and tackle all day for him. Imagine if all the players loved the coach and the effort they would then put in for him. Over to you, coach

– look after your players and they will look after you. By the way, they still have to be good players though!

243. Confidence can be built by giving the players small but achievable tasks, and then following this up with high praise. Once achieved, move the task to a higher level, watch for success, then praise again. This gradual improvement will need patience but the end result can see players grow so much in stature and produce performances you and they didn't think they were capable of.

244. Confident players know that defeats are part of life and these setbacks can further motivate them. Top players have a constant level of high confidence and this does not go up or down. Players with low confidence experience a rollercoaster of emotions, with their confidence levels going up and down. If they play one match well they are on a high, but if their next performance is not so good their confidence dives.

245. The player who can play brilliantly in every outfield position has not been produced yet. So we should be happy in what we do well and try to improve our strengths to a higher level. We can also have a 'work in progress' mentality where we gradually chip away to improve weaker parts of our game. Be confident that you have good attributes that not everybody possesses and that your effort and work rate on a football pitch are skills in their own right.

246. Every player has a different personality and a different confidence and self-worth level. Players can really feel happier when the coach takes them aside and praises them with positive feedback. The player will feel good that the coach has taken the time and effort to thank them for their effort and values them as a person and as a team player. If your confidence has been dented, having a conversation with a trusted friend, team-mate or coach can put you back on track quickly. Do not allow this brief lack of confidence to go further down by not taking action. Talking with the right people and giving yourself daily verbal pats on the back will work wonders and your confidence will return.

247. As a coach, it is a good idea to give your players a regular written report on their performances in training and matches. Keep it very positive, focus on strengths and end with a positive comment on their personality, for example 'John is very popular with his team-mates'. You can also suggest areas where improvement can be worked upon. It is a good idea to send a player a birthday or a Christmas card with a little comment expressing your thanks for all their efforts and telling them how well they are doing. They will arrive at the next training session refreshed and raring to go and they will appreciate the coach's thought.

248. Keep talking to yourself and giving yourself praise firstly for the effort you are putting in, secondly for the dedication you give, and thirdly for your performances. Self confidence is basically the result of our previous positive experiences. We have performed consistently well in a particular situation and repeating this performance has become the 'norm' for us. Tell yourself you are proud of your attitude and that you are a happy, well-balanced individual. Confidence is not arrogance. Arrogant people are unpopular and people smile when arrogant people are brought back down to earth with a bump. Real self confidence is having an inner belief but not outwardly telling people how good you are. Tell yourself 'I can do that' and work out what steps you need to take to achieve your goals.

249. Every individual on this planet loves to receive praise. From a small child to a tough-skinned world leader, we all feel much better if somebody says a simple 'well done' or 'thank you for all of your good work'. Football is a confidence-driven game, and the more a coach or a team-mate tells you how good you are, the more they are benefiting through your increasing confidence. So, coaches and players, say 'well done' a lot more than you are currently doing and watch the whole team's performance improve.

250. Confident players are not afraid to put their hands up and say 'Sorry, my mistake'. Players lacking in confidence and self esteem tend to blame others for their mistakes. This is a sign of their insecurity. It is important to take responsibility for an error and to do it immediately – either at half-time or at the end of the match. This prompt admission will not only give you increased respect from your coach and team-mates, but they will actually help you get over the mistake. They will admire you more and next time they might even copy you and take responsibility for their mistakes.

251. When a coach or manager joins a club there is a good chance that they are there because the previous manager has failed and the team are struggling. Not many managers take over an achieving team. A new coach should obviously address the immediate concerns of the team he has inherited but he should also give the players not in the team a boost by telling them individually that providing that they work very hard he will work with them to boost their confidence and give them an opportunity. Some of the current underperforming team could do with a rest and a player who has been frustrated by not playing could just be the newly motivated player to successfully take their opportunity. Many coaches and managers ignore the players not in the first-team 16-man match squad. They destroy their confidence by blanking them and they hardly say a word to them for weeks. A good coach will stay focused on all his players and will use this 'frustrated energy' to give a player a chance to cement his place in the team. By keeping all the players 'alive' keeps them on their toes and does not allow complacency to creep in. If a player does not want to play for the club or the manager then it is a good idea for the player to move on to another club and start again.

CONCENTRATION

252. Switch off for a second in football and your opponents have scored a goal, and possibly the winning goal. You lost concentration for that moment and now your team-mates are looking at you for an explanation. You would think that it would be easy to just focus for the length of a football match however some players struggle to do that. Concentration can be taught however, and with practise it can become a habit. You have to be motivated to learn concentration but the rewards in sport can be worth the effort.

Top footballers and sportspeople talk of 'being in the zone' where their total mental focus is to achieve a positive result. Being focused means putting everything in your life aside for the duration of the match. Concentrating just before the match can mean visualising your previous successes and imagining your mental state when you produced your best performances. Were you wound up or were you relaxed? Tense, worried players tend to carry previous mistakes to the next match but mentally relaxed players in the zone, can blank out previous mistakes immediately and focus on dealing with the next move of the current match. The positive ones can 'feel' the closeness of the ball as they control it perfectly, and distribute it accurately.

MOTIVATION

'You can not complete the goal unless you believe in it.'
JIM FURYK, USA 2008 RYDER CUP GOLFER

253. I was introduced to a man who was a workaholic. His business was his passion and the more his company grew, the more his motivation grew until one day a huge competitor offered to buy his company. Financially it was an offer he could not refuse. As he walked out of the factory door for the last time, with a cheque for millions of pounds, he looked back and recalled the effort, energy and drive he had devoted to his business. His motivation to get out of bed every morning was there in his factory with the people he had employed.

After travelling the world for two years, staying in the best hotels and eating the best food the world's top chefs could provide, he said the only place he had left to visit was the moon. He had exhausted all the other travel opportunities. He and his wife had lost the motivation to travel and had become bored with their lives. They had money, but their basic fundamental need was missing. They knew it was hard work, but seeing successful projects being developed was what drove them on. They built a private hospital, formed a professional rugby league team and became directors in a number of companies. His wife even rejoined the company that they had sold for millions. Their very basic needs were now satisfied and they become happy, driven people again. The objective with children is to always make them feel as though they are doing well. If a child enjoys their football they will continue to play it.

254. We are all motivated by different things. It could be money, achieving promotion at work, wanting to be famous, having a great new car or simply being loved and appreciated – a which is a child's favourite answer. In football terms if you are a good player as a child and find it easy to learn and master new skills, you will probably practise for hours and hours to further improve your technique. Motivation is a never-ending job, and motivating children with praise, encouragement and enthusiasm is easily the best solution. Motivation using fear does not work and is unacceptable in football as far as children and youngsters are concerned. I once worked for a large company where our MD used fear as a motivational tool. It worked for a short time before people stopped responding to his rants and raves. He was forced out and we all stayed.

255. Motivation is an attitude. Motivation is the reason we do what we do. Motivated players work very hard on the pitch, and hard working players at all levels are appreciated and welcomed by their team-mates and coaches. Motivated players are driven by the need to reach the highest level of football that is achievable for their ability. This drive can create a very focused individual with a need to find out what is required to be the best they can be.

256. Motivated players find it difficult to understand less driven team-mates, and this can cause its own problems. While it is important to have motivated players, they have to be taught that not everybody shares this feeling and that they can play a major part in encouraging less skilled and less motivated players.

257. Motivated players should be encouraged as they make good captains. They want to lead by example and motivated players want to win. They want to win tackles, cover many yards on the pitch and give passionate verbal instructions to their team-mates.

258. If you have a team of motivated players who work hard to combine their skills then you have a great base from which to succeed. Skills do not work without effort and if your team does not put enough effort in, frustrating results will follow. Some highly motivated players can take defeat badly. They may openly criticise team-mates, which can lower that team-mate's confidence and cause the offender to be disliked by his team. Ensure that positive behaviour is rewarded, and it is more likely to be repeated.

259. Motivation is a very strong and physical word. It suggests energy, great effort, and emotional feelings. This stirring up of emotions can cause some stress, but we need levels of stress to get us up and active and in the correct emotional state to perform tasks to the best of our ability. Imagine a football manager on the touchline at junior football on a Sunday morning, or a Premier Division coach pumping his clenched fists asking for more effort from his team.

260. Young children can be encouraged and motivated to play football by being given early praise. Catch them doing something good and then give them huge praise. They will feel that this active achievement will motivate them to do more of the same to achieve more praise.

261. When a youngster enjoys physical activity, this is then followed by an energising and refreshing shower or bath. Then, having had a drink and a nice snack or a meal, they will feel good and healthy and this will further motivate them to repeat the action.

262. Young people want to impress their parents, their friends and their team-mates. This is great motivation for them and I often see players looking over to their parents for approval with a smile and a thumbs up.

263. Winning trophies, medals and certificates at school, or representing a school, town, district, county or country, really drives individuals forward, as does being an important part of a team, playing in front of a crowd, achieving a 'man of the match' award and enjoying winning the game, league or cup. Some players play for enjoyment while others play to win trophies or recognition from others.

264. The fear of failure or of losing a match can provide the motivation to work harder in training, to improve fitness and to perhaps improve in dead-ball situations such as corners, free kicks and even with throw-in tactics. The more we are motivated to practise, the more likely it is that success will follow. Repetition will bring more success.

265. Youngsters love competition and I use it all the time at my academy. In a warm-up session, I put small groups up against each other and I tell them which group has performed the best and which individual was the best performer within the winning group. This works for all my age groups from five to 19 years old. This mild competition focuses their attention to do well, keep their concentration and beat the other groups. They are motivated when the skill they are asked to achieve is within their ability range but is a good test for them.

266. It is important in these little competitions in training that you, as the coach, want your players to achieve their goals and that they know it. Both the winning team and the best individual will be praised and the non-winners (I never say 'losers') will receive applause for the effort that they have put into the task. It is very important that effort is always rewarded with praise whether the team or player has won or not. Create the correct learning environment and challenge players at their level will bring both focus and motivation.

267. A smile from a coach, teacher or a parent, a thumbs up, or a high five now that's what I call a motivation to achieve more. As a child, a youngster, a youth and an adult the same words always motivated me. 'Well done, Paul, you are doing well'. It could have been my parents, a teacher, a coach, my managing director or my family. It still works today, it is my motivation. Perhaps I have an inner need to seek approval – what I do know is that when somebody says these words I want to do more, not less. People have been kind enough to say these words and I want to reward them with more of the same. What is your motivation, what drives you forward? Sit down and really think and work out what pleases you.

268. Planned, agreed objectives motivate us. It could be a task that sees you competing against yourself, such as completing more successful passes in a match. It could be that a defence decides not to allow attackers to turn so easily, or it could be wide players concentrating on delivering the ball more quickly and more accurately into agreed areas of the pitch. Measuring yourself against the required task is a good motivational tool.

269. Parents, coaches and teachers play a big part in the motivation and encouragement of young players. They know that all children are different and are motivated by different things. Your enthusiasm, drive and passion can rub off on them and the interest you take in them will provide supportive motivation to make them happy footballers.

As a coach, put a mini-questionnaire to each parent asking them what motivates their child, what their child most enjoys about football, and whether they practise at home. Have you considered giving out football homework? This sporting homework could give the youngsters a refreshing break from their school homework. You may even give the parents a guide for which skills to practise at home. Any extra time practising control and skills is going to benefit players on match day.

270. A player who has lower athletic ability but who loves their football must be motivated to improve with constant praise. Individual practise with the ball will improve their performance as will activities to improve their co-ordination, agility, balance and general movement and running style. Players who are a little overweight only need the 'praise motivation' for them to train more, and this combined with some tweaks to their eating habits will soon trim them down. While they train with the ball they forget that they are working hard and this is so much better than long distance running to lose weight. Any drop in weight will see their football improve and make them feel fitter, with boosted energy. What better motivation is there?

271. Casual players who like to play occasionally need to play in a group or a team where they can compete. To keep them actively involved they must receive plenty of touches in training and in matches and they need recognition from the coach and their team-mates. They need to feel wanted. If the level of football is too high and competitive for a player they could struggle, be discouraged and could be lost to football forever. Parents need to seek out a team who is playing at a level where your youngster can compete happily and comfortably.

272. Fear of failure is a big motivational factor. That is what drives many sports people and business people forward, but it does not work for everybody and should not be used with children. The motivation of earning lots of money can be huge, but what drives rich sportspeople to continue to want to win is their inner competitive spirit. They are used to winning and it has become a habit that they want again and again. Many people ask why the Rolling Stones still perform when they have all their super riches. The simple answer is that the money is secondary as they love the buzz that performing with their pals in front of huge audiences gives them. The same goes for sportspeople, especially the top successful ones, who are used to winning and playing to big crowds of adoring fans. When their careers are over there must be a big void left in their lives. When a group of talented sportspeople come together and they have this drive and collective motivation anything is possible. They have the motivational belief.

273. I have experienced being in a professional team that was expected to easily win an FA Cup match against a team from a division three leagues below ourselves. We were Hartlepool United and they were Runcorn. On the day we played, the weather was very cold, and we had a coach drive of three hours. Our local newspapers were talking about how many goals we would score and which players would score them. Runcorn were part-timers and the players worked in various jobs during the week from decorators to plumbers to firemen. They had played four matches to reach this round of the cup and this was our first cup match. Their average crowd was only 350 for home games and for many of these players this was their biggest match ever, in front of a crowd of nearly 4,000 very vocal supporters. This was their cup final and we misjudged what this meant to them. To us it was just another match. As we arrived at the ground 70 minutes before kick-off the reception we received from the home fans was, let's say, hostile. The changing rooms were built out of wood, they were crowded and there was no heating. Their supporters were banging on the windows and the wooden walls. The pitch had clearly not had any attention that week and it had been watered to make it worse. Everything was set up to distract us and we knew the first tackles we received would be aggressive. We knew that if we did not match their work rate and motivation, it would be them and not us going into the next round of the cup. After going 1-0 down just before half-time, we knew that we had to match their work rate and aggressiveness if we were going to salvage at least a draw. With a pitch that cows wouldn't be to happy to graze on we luckily scored in the last couple of minutes to achieve a replay which we won at home 4-1.

I also played for Hartlepool United in an FA Cup match against First Division opposition in Crystal Palace. This time they were the clear favourites and their team had a number of full internationals. I watched as they arrived at our dilapidated ground and I sensed that they were not focused on the match. Our levels of excitement were intense and we couldn't wait to get out there to prove our ability. Our team was made up of players who hadn't really achieved at a higher level but we had the hunger to achieve a cup shock. As they got ready in the changing room, which had only had its mouse traps removed an hour earlier, we smiled at the thought of their faces on that crisp early January afternoon as they realised that the heater had unfortunately just broken.

Our ground was packed full, the atmosphere was electric and after our first tackles hit the mark we saw in their eyes that they were not up for the battle. Our players wanted to win more than their players.

As our winning goal went in, we knew we deserved our 2-1 victory. They were a team beaten before the kick off. Ability without motivation does not achieve anything.

PASSION

'Passion is the best word in sport, and this event drags the passion out of you like nothing else.'

IAN WOOSNAM BEFORE HIS 2006 EUROPEAN TEAM
BEAT THE USA IN THE RYDER CUP GOLF

274. We have all seen the international player who has received a cut on the head and who returns to the field to play on wearing a bandage soaked in blood. That's passion, as is the team and fans who sing their country's national anthem before a big match, or the athlete on the winning podium as they accept a gold medal with a tear in their eye and a lump in their throat.

275. Passion is a feeling, a belief, it is a pride word, it is something that can bring a countries people together and unite them in a common theme or an interest. Passion is a fantastic motivational tool, and a very powerful motivational word. Passionate people who have talent, and who are driven and dedicated to their objective, are winners.

MENTAL TOUGHNESS

'A mentally tough player will be self motivated and
will only need mild encouragement from the coach
to fulfil his work rate, he will only think about
positive outcomes for every second of the match.'

276. Parents, family and friends are the ones who support a child. Then that child joins a local academy or junior club and the coach becomes a mentor to them. At this stage, early signs of their levels of mental strength can be detected. Each training session, a player will receive a knock of some kind and it is interesting to see how they react to this situation. Some children will want you to see the injury; some will feel distressed and will want to come off the pitch; others will just want to get back into the match without delay.

Just by talking to the child you can assess their attitude and begin to see their personal strength. A coach can work on the individual's mentality by giving them praise following a strong tackle or a determined driving surge forward. It is important to understand that players can drop out of football because they are not as mentally strong or as physically capable as other players in the group.

277. It's easy to think that mentally tough players are the big, aggressive, combative players who are loud and sometimes difficult to control. Well yes, I know where you are coming from, but sometimes the toughest one can be a quiet player who can be cool and calculating and know what he wants. Beware of the quiet, motivated ones – they will arrive on the scene unexpectedly and have an instant impact.

278. There are a lot of different characters and personalities in every team game, and in every sport. It is good to have a mix, with happy, laughing, outgoing, optimistic people and players who do not say a lot but who contribute with constant good performances. It is possible to give the impression that you are a mentally tough player even though inside you are not. To do this, though, you have to be the leader and produce consistent performances where you have to have a 'tackle a brick wall' mentality. You can be a pleasant person off the pitch, but on the pitch turn into dominant warriors for your team.

279. Some players can really come to life when they are playing a team from a higher division and they love the challenge of a cup tie against a team that's expected to win easily. This challenge can provide great excitement; however the same player will find playing a team a few leagues below them in the cup, or a league match against a team bottom of the league, a real de-motivation. That's why cup shocks happen. The top teams think the job is easy and can turn up expecting to put in minimum effort. For the lower league team, this is their big day, their 'cup final', and they can't wait to topple the big guns. They train even harder, prepare better than ever, and they go to sleep dreaming of victory and visualising the faces of the beaten primadonnas. Obviously it is up to the bigger team's manager to motivate and prepare his players for every game and avoid embarrassing slip-ups, which do happen. As football fans, don't we just love it when an upset occurs!

280. Mentally tough players love a challenge and when problems occur they see this as an opportunity to shine. They soon work out who the mentally tough players in their team are and also on the opposing team. Mentally tough players have a real belief in their ability, and nothing or nobody will shake off this inner belief.

281. The cool, self-controlled, mentally tough player will never give up on the pitch, but he will also never lose his composure or lose control or push or hit anyone. The physically strong and less controlled mentally tough player may make a tackle that he knows could get him booked or sent off and this player needs to be watched. It should be explained to him that his attitude and behaviour may have a negative impact on the team.

282. A mentally strong, thinking player will cover all angles to make sure that they are a vital player in the team. They will understand that they must be at their very best in terms of physical fitness and have a dedicated and focused mentality. They will know that to be at their physical peak they have to eat the correct food and have plenty of sleep and rest.

283. While defeat is hard to accept, the mentally strong player knows when he has not performed to his best. He will work harder to produce a better performance in the next game. He knows that being a stop-start, inconsistent player is not enough, and that he will be judged on his overall performances at the end of the season.

284. Mentally tough players are there to win the match. They want to win every training match and every competitive game they participate in. They are a shining example to others and they lead by example in difficult times. They will continue to want the ball even when they have made a mistake as they want to put that mistake right. They will want the ball when other team-mates do not; however good players will encourage their team-mates, giving them encouragement to express themselves. A couple of wins in a row can make a huge difference and this new-found confidence can propel the team on to an extended run of victories.

285. Mistakes are part of football and it is crucial that players remember this and work out options to minimise errors and mistakes. Mentally strong players do not worry about making mistakes as they know this is part of football. They know they are good players and that a high proportion of their play on the field is very good and productive. In difficult times they know their continued hard work will eventually produce positive results. This type of player is not afraid to 'want the ball' in any situation, including difficult games where his team are having confidence-sapping results. This player is a 'rock'.

286. There can be many distractions in a player's life both on and off the pitch, but the tough, mentally focused players put all these problems out of their minds as they focus in the 'concentration zone'. They know that a training session will normally last for less than two hours and a match for even fewer minutes, so they consider that in a 24-hour day this is only a very short zone or period of time where their whole passion and concentration is required. There are 168 hours in a full week and a mentally tuned player knows that 90 minutes of match concentration can provide him with great rewards.

WINNING MENTALITY

'The winning mentality is very important– if you play with fear it is impossible to win.'

FABIO CAPELLO

287. Winning a match and being part of the team that has worked so hard to achieve a win is a great feeling. Children are told 'it's the taking part that counts' – yes that's okay but the pleasure of winning far outweighs the taking part and getting beaten, and the confidence that winning gives. If a child takes part and gets beaten every time his confidence will be shot and there is a very good chance that he will leave this sport.

288. As the great Liverpool manager Bob Paisley used to say, 'Losing or coming second is like living next door to the pools winner'. In other words, who remembers the runner-up? If you ask children which teams have won the Premier League or the FA Cup they can tell you the winners going back ten years or more, but they find it difficult to name the runners up.

289. Focus and commitment, and the correct positive mental attitude, form the basis for winning football matches. If you have to want to win matches, you have to want to train hard to be physically strong and you have to get on with your team-mates. If everybody has this will and desire, it is amazing what can be achieved.

290. The mind is very powerful. If you tell yourself constantly that you are very good at something then eventually you will start to believe it. I was never the best swimmer and if I simply told myself I was good nothing would happen. However, if I took lessons and worked at the correct techniques on a regular basis I could then start to tell myself I was good and this would motivate me even more to improve.

291. Be good at what you do and tell yourself how brilliant you are. We all talk to ourselves in our heads – it is called thinking. We do it all of our waking lives. We talk to ourselves as we wake up and clean our teeth and have our breakfast. We talk as we go to school or to work. We look at people and in our heads we decide whether we like their looks or what clothes they are wearing. Some people think negative thoughts about themselves and have doubts about their abilities.

Tomorrow, though, could see you thinking positive thoughts. Tell yourself that you will enjoy the 'now'; that every second of every day you will try to make it a happy and positive time. When you open your mouth, listen very carefully to what you are saying and how you are saying it. Keep everything positive. Smile much more than you normally do, and ask people how they are and tell them how well they look. Over the four weeks, write down how you felt and how people reacted to you. It needs practise but tell yourself how unique you are on this planet. It is true: there is only one you. Tell yourself you are doing well in life and that you intend to make every day a good one.

After all, it is YOUR life and, as my gran used to say, if you live to 100 years old it is not a long time. So welcome to your new 'now' – enjoy life!

SUCCESS

'Successful is the person who has lived well, laughed often and loved much, and who has gained the respect of children, who leaves the world better than they found it and who never fails to look for the best in others or give the best of themselves.'

AUTHOR UNKNOWN

292. We can get used to feeling confident and get used to winning. Make winning and competing an everyday part of your life. Set yourself tasks that you can achieve, then once one thing is achieved and mastered, set the level higher. Winning is a positive mentality and a mentality that you can teach yourself. You can decide how your mind will react to whatever happens in your life today. Walk into school or college or work and give three compliments to people during the day. Watch their reaction to the compliment and think about how you felt giving the compliment and how you felt when you saw their happy reaction. Tomorrow, be positive about everything – including the weather – and again watch people's reactions. Learn to pick two positives from every negative situation you come across.

293. Winning and losing are habits. Study teams that are top of their league in every sport. There is a good chance that the top teams have had a run of wins that has created a winning mentality. When they run out onto the pitch they are expecting to win again. It is in their mind that they have done it before and they know what it takes to do it again. This team has a collective strength and a belief to extend the winning habit. The team's body language is confident, strong and upright.

294. The teams at the bottom of the league have the losing habit and they do not have a clue how they or their team-mates are going to perform. They have forgotten how to win and they do not have confidence in their team's current form or mentality. Mentally they are weakened by poor results and individually they struggle to accept responsibility for their actions, sometimes blaming others which can further erode the team spirit. Players are not confident in receiving the ball, so they put themselves in a position where it is difficult for a team-mate to pass to them. A change of players in the spine of the team will help, making sure that positive leaders are introduced, which will change the mindset of the team.

295. You hear it said that 90% of sporting performance is between the ears (in your mind), and 10% is ability. That rough statement does tell us the importance of positive thinking. It is all linked, as is winning and losing. That's why it is important to get the right mix of players in your team. They can have many different blends of skills; however, if the team as a group is not mentally strong then you have a problem.

296. Setting targets and objectives is important to stimulate a winning team. In children it is okay to ask them to improve a skill – passing technique or style, for example. For children in junior teams it is a good idea to set short term objectives, say increasing the number shots at goal, or winning the ball back quickly when the team loses possession, or seeing how many crosses the players can deliver into the penalty area. In older players, objectives could be aimed at both the team or at individuals. The team plan could be for the team to push out quickly to the halfway line when attacking, or individual players might be asked to focus on achieving three accurate passes in a row and repeating this action throughout the match.

Ensure that these targets and objectives are not too easy or too hard and that you have taken into consideration the age and ability of your team and the opposition. Achievement of the targets will give confidence and boost self esteem.

If the targets are set mid- to long-term, youngsters tend to focus on them and lose concentration on their immediate and short-term goals. Congratulate your players in front of their team-mates.

'The person who risks nothing, does nothing, sees nothing, has nothing and is nothing. He cannot learn, feel, change, grow, love and live.'

AUTHOR UNKNOWN

VISUALISATION AND IMAGINATION

297. In my football and business life I often picture in my mind what the outcome will be if I put certain actions into place. As a 12-year-old I imagined what it would be like to play in the first team at Manchester United. Within five years I achieved that goal. I imagined what it would be like to proudly walk out onto the pitch wearing the three England lions on my shirt. I achieved this playing in Switzerland in the England Youth team.

In business I visualised what I wanted to achieve and absolutely dedicated myself to achieve it. Again I was successful, but I was driven and all the extra hours I had to work were worth the commitment.

298. Once you understand the power of visualisation you will see that all footballers, from children to youngsters to adults, can make this tool a great asset in their success.

Think back into your memory box and see all of the success you have enjoyed. Remember what you did very well. It could have been the feeling of achieving a great win, or a perfectly-timed shot at goal, or a great pass that absolutely pinged off your foot. As a goalkeeper, was it an acrobatic diving save or when you bravely dived at the attacker's feet? If you do something really well, store it in your memory. When you need to release it, bring the memory forward to repeat the success you previously achieved.

299. Positive visualisation is dreaming of doing great things. Many years on, I can still feel the ball as it left my foot to score my best ever goal. Everything felt right; my body and arms were well balanced and I timed the ball perfectly off my foot. It was a sweet moment and as soon as I made contact with the ball I knew it was going to take a great save to stop it. I can still see my team-mates' reaction and time seemed to move in slow-motion. I could take you to the exact spot where I made contact with the ball.

300. Top sportspeople use visualisation, especially golfers. As they decide which club to take for the required distance, they mentally picture the type of shot required and how the ball will react to the weather conditions and the contours on the green. Footballers do this, especially when taking dead-ball kicks. Free kick experts can replicate their body shape from previous memories of goals scored. They can see in their mind's eye how they should strike the ball to achieve a successful outcome. They have practised this technique thousands of times and they can visualise the required outcome.

301. A parent or a coach could really improve their youngsters' style and technique by using a video camera to show the youngsters' current style and show them where improvement and changes can be made. A DVD showing a gifted professional rich in technique could be purchased and a youngster could copy his role model's style. The player could then see his own efforts on screen, which would very quickly improve his skill acquisition.

302. Confidence and visualisation are linked. All top matches are now televised so the players have a constant reminder of that great skill that they have achieved. They can build a collection of their own personal hits and sit down and see the action over and over to prove how good they are.

The more they see their success the more confident they become to repeat it.

'What we can easily see is only a small percentage of what is possible. Imagination is having the vision to see what is just below the surface, to picture that what is essential, but invisible to the eye.'

FOOTBALL AGGRESSION.

'Give 100% in everything you do and never give up.'

303. There are players in every team who are the physical guys, who do the dirty work to provide the foundations for the gifted players to be creative to score or make the goals. The aggression I am talking about in this observation, though, is mental aggression as opposed to physical aggression. There are players who are very quiet off the pitch; the ones who you never hear complain and, in fact, who you hardly hear talk. However, this quietness can hide a drive that can be much stronger and powerful than the brash, outgoing, demonstrative person.

This type of player can be seen by others as having a laid back attitude and not being that motivated. BEWARE. This player can be the quiet assassin of the team, who trains, plays, wins and then goes home to a quiet life. They are motivated by the win.

304. The physical tackling side of football has a much softer edge now than it did in the 1960s, '70s and '80s. The tackles then were very cynical and each team had its very obvious hatchet man. The Laws of the Game allowed for more physical contact, including barging the goalkeeper. A player receives much more protection now and you can hardly look at a goalkeeper without receiving a yellow card. Tackling in football is an art form and is a football skill in its own right that can be improved with practise. It is one of those skills that coaches rarely teach and most of the time it is left to the players to teach themselves. Perhaps coaches think that they only want to improve the pretty skills and not the ugly ones. A physically aggressive player has to have 'the want' to play this way, but when they get it right this category of player could be the manager's first pick every time.

305. Players wind themselves up for the match in different ways. The coach will say to the team before the match 'win your individual physical battle first 'and then play your football. Basically he means make sure that your first physical encounter or tackle is won as this sets the scene for the rest of the match. It shows your opponent how you feel about the match and how motivated you are. When I was at Hartlepool United we had two big aggressive centre forwards called Bob Newton and Terry Turnbull. Both were good players but they were also battering rams. At the first opportunity in every match they would make it very clear to the opposing central defenders that they were in for a bad day and that they would they would visit them in hospital after the match.

They were the minders in the team and we knew it. We used to knock high passes into them and then try and be around them as they won the ball and left the poor struggling defender on the floor. Both players were popular with the supporters as they are characters and 'effort' players. Fans have a sense of receiving value for money when they see players giving every last effort for their team.

306. Aggression in the mind is key as this is an aggressive contact sport where winning in professional football is the only acceptable option. As footballers we are all different; however we all have to walk out onto that football field with the correct mental attitude, and there are so many ways of making sure that your mind is focused at kick off time. Some players listen to aggressive rock music on their personal headsets, others have an ice-cold shower to wake themselves up. Some have rituals that they perform before each game such as putting their kit on in the same order or going onto the pitch in the same order in the team. There are players who will just want to be left alone to wind themselves up and others that find that winding other players up also motivates themselves. Photographs of their loved ones are kept by players to look at just before kick off to give them that that final 'bite' to compete. Some teams have a team hug before they play where the captain or coach gives the final motivational blast, and they aggressively shake hands before the warriors compete.

MAKING MISTAKES

307. Making mistakes are part of life; it is how we react to mistakes and how quickly we recover from them that shapes our character.

Very confident footballers do not even think about the mistakes they make they just move on to the next phase of play. The top players work on minimising errors, however they know that we are all human and that mistakes happen. Players lacking confidence and self esteem can dwell on their mistakes and errors and as each mistake is compounded their confidence escapes from them. A positive coach will recognise this weakness and try to put it right by given huge praise to this type of player and many individual conversations will correct the fault and make the player want to play for this appreciating manager.

'Don't worry about making mistakes: they are the price we pay for living a full life.'

CHAPTER 7

School Football

'The first time I went to school and played football the teacher we had was great fun, he made it enjoyable and we had a great laugh. When the session was over we always wanted more. That's a good coach.'

KEVIN KEEGAN

PRIMARY SCHOOLS

308. In primary schools a high proportion of teachers are female and this has an effect on learning and coaching football. While some female teachers enjoy taking football, the majority do not. It is to their credit, however, that they will take the team as nobody else will and the children could otherwise miss out. Many primary schools now hire coaches to come into school during the day to help coach football and sporting skills.

309. If you are a male teenager reading this book and you love football and sport in general, I would recommend that you work towards qualifying to be a primary school teacher. In the UK, male teachers are an endangered species as only one in 50 primary school teachers are male and one in 10 schools have no male teachers at all. At a time when many children live in single-parent families, usually with just their mother at home, more and more kids have little or no contact with a male role model. You could have a job for life, particularly with an ability to coach and organise sporting activities. Secondary schools are generally well catered for, with up to six qualified male and female sports teachers at one school.

I would also encourage sports-mad females to go into primary school teaching, especially if they also gain coaching awards in a number of sports. They will enjoy their normal educational teaching but the sporting side will make them real heroes with the children. Be prepared to take after-school sports lessons and team coaching sessions and your head teacher and parents will think you are a star. There are so few female primary school teachers who understand and coach football that you will be a real asset to your school.

310. While secondary schools have good-sized sports halls for indoor activities on bad weather days, primary schools often only have multi-purpose halls, which are not big enough or suitable for robust sports such as football and rugby. These halls double up as school assembly halls, dinner halls and are also used for sport. I have seen many where the hall is surrounded by stacked-up chairs or where a full-sized piano stands proudly in the corner. Health and safety and space issues are a problem, especially compounded with a class of 30-plus boys and girls crammed into an area where the teacher is hoping to provide a meaningful 60-minute sports lesson.

311. Nothing is more important to a parent than the health of their children. As schools have to provide a minimum of two hours of physical activity each week, it is important that you as a parent check to see which activities your children are taking part in, how often, and how many children are supervised by each teacher. It would be a good idea for you to ask to be present at an indoor and then an outdoor PE lesson.

What you could find in the hour-long lesson is that it will take the children 15 minutes to arrive from their previous lesson and then get changed, then after 30 minutes of low-intensity activity they are told to go inside, get changed (nobody showers) and be ready for their next lesson or break time. Parents are told that the children receive X hours of sports lessons per week but the reality when it comes to 'quality' time is often very different.

312. Let the primary school know that physical activity is very important to you as a parent. Also ask to see what qualifications and experience the teachers currently have to teach, organise and coach sport. Do not feel guilty asking for this information. It makes sure that the school has a focus on providing quality, meaningful and beneficial sporting lessons. If the head teacher complains about the quality of their sporting facilities, then it is up to them to campaign for better facilities. Usually the ones that shout loudest and longest are rewarded with the finances to upgrade their schools.

313. We must understand that not all pupils are academically minded and therefore do not enjoy school. What they do often enjoy, though, is sport and they are often good at it. These pupils should be given the same encouragement in their sport as the academically gifted pupils. Sport can bring these kids alive and stir their enthusiasm and passion.

314. If you believe that you are better qualified than the teachers to offer quality coaching, I am sure that you will be made very welcome. Why not offer to give a couple of free sessions where the teacher or head teacher can assess you to see if you are suitable? Watching the happy faces of the youngsters will provide evidence of your organising and simply making the kids happy skills. After these trial sessions the school could even be a position to pay you.

315. In my home town of Darlington, I formed our Primary School Football Association 10 years ago, as there had been no organised inter-school football leagues and cups for over 30 years. After discussions with Janet Cooper, the local council's Sports Development Officer, I wrote to the 32 primary schools in the area, but only four showed any genuine interest. I then put the details in the local press and parent power encouraged other schools to take part. We started a boys' league and annual cup day with 26 teams.

In these last 10 years, thousands of children have enjoyed the thrill of representing their schools and this recognition will stay in their memories for the rest of their lives.

I further introduced an indoor five-a-side cup which takes place in November each year and a seven-a-side cup in May each year. Hundreds of primary school pupils play in these competitions.

I introduced the Primary School Girls' League and Cup competitions in 2004 and the girls are absolutely thrilled with this opportunity to play competitive football. I invited a friend, Tony Cox, who had achieved so much success with junior teams and the Cubs, to help me and he and I coach a district boys' representative team and now we have a district girls' football team who play teams from Durham, Northumberland and Yorkshire. All this work is unpaid and voluntary but it has given me as much pleasure as playing for Manchester United and representing England at youth level.

316. There is lots of evidence to show that children who exercise on a regular basis also do very well in the classroom. Fit children feel happier, sleep better, have improved concentration levels and are able to study longer and have improved results. Research also confirms that they are more confident individuals with positive self esteem.

317. An Ofsted report stated that a quarter of secondary schools in England have a shortage of playing fields and even when schools do have pitches they are often waterlogged and gyms are frequently run down. This has meant that sport now has diminished importance in the school curriculum.

Ofsted warned that conditions need to be improved if young people are to achieve the high levels expected. In too many schools the emphasis is simply in taking part in PE rather than developing a body of knowledge and skills associated with health and fitness. Shabby changing rooms also put kids off sporting participation.

According to statistics, many pupils arriving at secondary schools in year 7 are unfit for exercise.

318. Less than two-thirds of pupils receive two hours of physical education per week. One reason is that almost half of school playing fields have been sold off in the last 16 years.

SECONDARY SCHOOLS

The range of sports to play at secondary school is fantastic compared with junior school. The facilities are much better and the teachers are full-time trained specialists. Talented sports players now have an opportunity to earn a place in a school team, a town and district team and even a county or national team. As the teachers are specialists who know their subject well, they can advise on the best sport for each individual's ability and they will encourage students to achieve sporting grades to go alongside academic achievements.

319. School teachers become real heroes in the lives of children if they help them develop their football skills and select them for the school team. The youngsters see themselves as representing every child in their school and it gives them tremendous pride. They are respected by their classmates and the younger ones aspire to be like them. I can still remember looking out of the window at school, waiting to see our opponents arrive. I can still feel the material of the kit on my skin and the clean smell of it. The energy was huge as we stepped on to the pitch and the smell of the newly-mown grass attracted my keen senses, as did the white line markings. A 2-1 win over Abbey with Rod Humble scoring the winner from my crisp pass capped a day I would still remember clearly 42 years later. I could hardly wait for the next match.

320. Secondary school sport is delivered by specialist teachers who are trained experts in their field. Most have been university educated and have achieved a sports-related degree. Football is recognised as the first-choice sport in most schools and the teachers are well equipped to coach, manage and select a school team. As girls' football is now recognised as sport's fastest-growing sport, female teachers are now more qualified to coach and then there is now a growing number of girls getting involved.

321. There are much more sporting options at secondary school for both boys and girls and the facilities are far superior to those at primary schools. Most secondary schools have a dedicated sports hall and some have a swimming pool, athletics track and all-weather facilities. At most primary schools the pupils do not shower after sport as there are no facilities available, but at secondary schools there are showers and proper changing rooms for the lads and lasses.

322. Football matches against other schools at both primary and junior school level are much more relaxed compared with Sunday morning junior football. Teachers control the atmosphere, referee the matches and will simply not allow on or off the field sportsmanship, to occur which can happen in junior football occasionally.

323. In England, The English Schools' Football Association does an excellent job of organising football at both primary and secondary school level. At a local level, competitions are organised by the County Schools' Football Association. In each county, representative teams are selected from each district at primary level and different age groups at secondary level. These district teams play league and cup matches against other district teams, and if successful, go on to play in regional finals and then into national finals.

CHAPTER 8

Junior Football Clubs

Junior football clubs have a very important part to play in the local community and are organised by very caring, dedicated, unpaid volunteers who give many hours of hard work to ensure that youngsters enjoy their sport. These fantastic people do a great job.

FINDING A CLUB

324. It is both an exciting time and a nervous time when a youngster joins a junior football club. It is a good idea to take Junior to watch the team train before you decide to join them and to watch both a home and an away match. Watching this activity will give you an insight into the style of environment that your child will be joining.

You as a parent can check to see if all of the players were individually greeted on their arrival at training – did they look happy and motivated during the training session? Was the coach organised and enthusiastic and did he give lots of praise to his players? On match day did the coach give the subs enough playing time and was he positive in winning and losing situations?

325. Appearance and body language is important and our initial opinion of someone is based on what we see and hear. The coach has so much influence on your child's football experience so it is key that they look well dressed and that they display positive body language with a friendly nature. They could be an important role model in your youngster's future for a number of years so the coach must have attributes that you are happy for your youngsters to copy; i.e. enthusiasm, humour, a sense of fun and fairness, compassion for others and a passion for football.

326. Parents and spectators are key people in junior football but sometimes their enthusiasm can be disruptive and spoil a happy event for all concerned.

Parents and spectators must understand that this is football for children and that they are there to give praise, support and encouragement to the young players. Applaud and appreciate good play by the opposition and if the referee has had a good game tell him so at the end. Do not complain to him if he has had a bad game.

327. Have you had a look at a number of clubs in your area? It is also a good idea to speak to parents of current players so that you can ascertain the club's good and bad points.

Does the club have a website? Are the current committee

well established and respected in the area, and does every-body have an up to date CRB (Criminal Records Bureau) certificate which is mandatory.

Does your youngster have any pals in the team who could help him settle in? This is such an important factor, especially for younger children who can be quite nervous. Having a pal there at the beginning helps them settle down and they can then make inroads into making new friends together. Can you see a copy of the club's code of conduct? Do the coaches have coaching qualifications and are they emergency first aid trained? How many coaches are there per team, and what are the views of the parents in your youngster's potential team?

Another important fact you will need to know is which league they are playing in and in which division. The players need to be competitive and therefore need to be in a league where they are enjoying a good proportion of wins and draws. Some defeats do little harm, as they need to experience this, but winning regularly gives everybody in the squad (and their parents) a lift, even if that means playing in a lower division.

Being top of Division 4 is a lot better than getting hammered every week in Division 1, where enjoyment and confidence will be in short supply. When everybody is positive there is always a good turnout at training and matches and a bounce in the players' step. When wins are a rare occurrence, players miss training and make excuses to miss matches, and the better players look to join better teams.

328. Once you have decided that this is the club and team for your youngster, it is now important that you meet the coach or manager to find out if he has a place in the squad for your child and whether he believes your child will be able to play a decent amount of match minutes.

As the coach selects the team, he will want to asses your child's ability and gauge their skills and ability against his current players.

From professional football down to grassroots level the coach will use the same measurement: 'Is this player better than the players we already have in our squad'? If the answer is yes, then your child will enjoy plenty of playing time. If the answer is no, then he will probably have little match time.

When a player is playing matches it is great fun but when he is sub and hardly gets any match time, it is really no fun at all. It is difficult for coaches to tell parents that their loved one is a squad member rather than a regular player, but you need to encourage the coach to give their honest opinion as this can save time and disappointments.

Some junior clubs have an A and a B team in an age group and it's much better to be playing every week in the B team than not playing many minutes in the A team. A child won't mind playing in the B team as long as he is playing regular matches; however parents' pride can be hurt as they see their child as being good enough to play in the A team. But youngsters need to play and enjoy their football with freedom, and experience the wins and defeats that develop their personalities.

SUPPORTING YOUR COACH

329. A coach has to decide whether he is going to select a team for enjoyment or whether he is building a team to win matches. There is a huge difference between the two options.

In selecting the team, the coach has to be fair to his best players by selecting his strongest team. Some managers/ coaches will pick a team that gives all the players equal playing time and won't worry too much about the result as long as it is a close game and everyone enjoys themselves. Some coaches will understand that the best players will want to win the game and he will decide on a strong line-up. But if a coach takes this option and gives everybody fair playing time, they can run the risk of losing their best players if good results do not follow. The best players usually want to win games and trophies, and they can find it difficult if they see good players on the subs bench and players with lesser skills starting the match.

Sometimes it is best for the coach not to bring all the allotted substitutes to a match. Some leagues allow five subs, but coaches know that if they give all five subs some match time the whole balance of the team can be severely disturbed. At junior clubs it is a very fine balancing act, and although the coach wants to please everyone it is not always possible.

330. Football is such an emotional game and match day brings a whole rollercoaster of emotions. Within seconds a game can change from a laid-back 0-0 draw to a win or lose situation and it is vital that the adults show consistent good behaviour that sets a good example to the youngsters present. Be confident in your coach and let him select the team and the players' positions and then motivate them to enjoy the match day experience.

331. Parents should focus on the good things that their youngster has done and tell them how proud they are of them. If the result has gone against them, or they have not had a good game, remind them of all their positive previous experiences and tell them to look forward to the next game. At all times maintain their love for the game.

332. Junior football is rich in enjoyment and not only will the players make new pals, but the parents will develop friendships to last a lifetime.

Some of the best occasions are at annual presentation evenings when all of the players receive an award, with the better performers winning player or sportsman of the season. To see a child receive their very first trophy is fantastic and a sight to cherish. There are many and varied events that clubs organise for parents to get together and these include fancy dress parties and sportsman or sportswoman dinners. You will look back in years to come and see that a number of your close friendships were formed on the touchline of muddy football pitches on a freezing cold Sunday morning as you drank your coffee or a fellow parent's much-welcomed hot soup.

333. Junior football clubs play an important part in the local community and they have a great opportunity to forge positive relationships with the local schools, youth clubs and church groups. Clubs will always need to raise funds to buy new playing kit, footballs and equipment and having a good relationship with your local superstore manager will help promote activities and boost funds.

Many junior clubs play on school playing fields so it is important that the club has a good relationship with whoever looks after the pitches. During the poor weather months teachers naturally they do not want their pitches to become unplayable in school time. Being sensible with vulnerable, poorly-drained pitches is a good idea and you should not risk damaging them for the short-term gain of having a match played. Postpone some matches if necessary and play them later in the season when the weather is good and the pitches are firm. Helping the school with fundraising is a good idea – perhaps painting and maintaining the changing rooms will be help your school/club relationship.

334. It's great when youngsters see their team's results in the local press, especially when they win or when a youngster grabs the headlines with the winning goal or man of the match performance. If you have an annual presentation evening (I would strongly recommend one) it's a good idea to ask your local newspaper editor to present the awards.

MANAGING A TEAM

335. As you are already there to watch your youngster train and play in matches, you could help out as secretary, treasurer, coach or manager. The feeling of being part of your team or club's success is brilliant and your youngster will be very proud.

Football is a game of opinions and as adults we sometimes think we could be good football coaches ourselves. If you believe this, then there is no time like the present. Put your name down with the club secretary and ask to be considered when a position becomes available. All you will initially need to do is put in for a CRB check, which will take about six weeks to come through, and ask if the club will put you on the next available coaching course to gain an officially recognised coaching qualification. While you are waiting for a position, visit a good bookstore and purchase a couple of coaching books which will show you coaching drills and skills.

I have seen people with no real initial interest in football go on to become chairman of a club. My friend and fellow coach Barry Dawson took an interest in the sporting injuries side of football and now works full time as a lecturer and is also a very well respected qualified physio and teacher for a number of county Football Associations.

My son's Cubs master, Tony Cox, suggested the idea for a junior football club and 14 years on the club has hundreds of players and Tony continues to manage our district team at 68 years of age with great enthusiasm and experience.

336. Coaching a team with your son or daughter in it can be a difficult one; however if your youngster is good enough to easily earn their place it makes life easier. There can be problems in a number of areas if you want your youngster in the team but they are not good enough to earn a regular start. If you play your son you will inevitably receive criticism from the other parents, particularly those whose children play in the same position as your child. If you do not play your son you will feel bad for him and guilty as he was probably the reason why you chose to become involved in the club in the first place. Oh yes, and you'll get stick from your wife for not selecting your lad!

337. The running of a junior football club is not only a male domain, as many clubs have a growing number of mums and grandmas who play key roles as committee members and in the very important fundraising sector. Established clubs now have girls' teams of various ages and these are coached and organised by both male and female coaches.

Some mums could never have foreseen that they would end up standing at the side of a football pitch on a freezing cold Sunday morning. But this is where lasting friendships can be made. Instead of Hubby taking Junior to the match, go as a family and your youngster will love it. Mums play a huge part in junior football and without them the games on Sunday mornings wouldn't have the same exciting atmosphere.

MINI-SOCCER
338. Until 1999, young children played 11-a-side matches on adult-sized pitches, using adult-sized goals. These youngsters hardly received a touch of the ball, ran distances

that their young frames were not really capable of and the poor goalkeeper looked lost between the huge goalposts.

Mini-soccer was created to make football much more attractive to children under 10 years of age. It works really well and with its simple rules it has proved to be a fantastic success. Mini-soccer is a cut-down version of adult soccer and it provides exciting end-to-end scoring opportunities. The best way for children and adults to enjoy the game is for adults to set it up and then stay quiet and be mesmerised at the children's enjoyment.

339. Players under 10 play mini-soccer – small-sided matches of seven-a-side – and these very entertaining games are played on smaller pitches (60 yards x 40 yards) with age-appropriate goals.

These games ensure that every player has more touches of the ball and gains experience of playing in a number of positions. With only seven players on a team each player has a part to play and they need to work together as a unit. They move forward together to score goals and they collectively work hard to win the ball and then retain it. This format helps them develop their football intelligence as they are often in situations that require them to make quick decisions. Do I pass the ball or shoot? Do I stay on my feet and delay the attacker until my team-mates arrive, or do I dive in to win the ball quickly?

There are many decisions to be made, and children will learn as they play more matches. These games provide end to end activity and many scoring opportunities which make these matches very exciting to watch. At times, these matches can be much more exciting than watching professional teams. These youngsters thrive on energy and enthusiasm and they have an honesty that is refreshing to see.

340. The match result, certainly at under-10 level, should not be the most important factor. Encouraging improved skills and enjoyment should be the objective. Striving for wins at all costs will restrict the players' creativity, and coaches shouting 'Pass the ball!' all the time will stop the players dribbling and performing the skills and tricks which they need to perfect to make them more valuable to the team.

CODES OF CONDUCT

341. In any organised group it is important to have rules or a code of conduct. This ensures that everybody is aware of the group's disciplinary requirements and therefore saves confusion. The objective is for everybody to be happy and to work together as a team to produce a happy and positive atmosphere for all. In football it is a good idea to have rules for the players, the spectators/parents and coaches and managers.

These rules need to be handed out at the beginning of each season and handed to new coaches, players and parents when they join the club.

Code of conduct for players
Accept wins and losses graciously and modestly
Never argue with the referee and match officials

Do what the referee tells you

You are allowed to tackle hard, but it must be within the rules

Maintain your self control and do not retaliate

Encourage your team-mates to play hard but fair

Play with enjoyment in your mind

Do not cheat and try to win penalties and free kicks etc that are not yours

Shake hands after the game with your team-mates and your opponents

Appreciate that you are representing your school/club

Thank your teachers, coaches or manager and thank the referee

Code of conduct for parents/spectators

Enjoy the match

Cheer and applaud your team

Appreciate the opponent's good play

Do not give instructions to players during the match

Do not argue with the match officials. Show a good example

After the match, applaud both teams and thank the match officials

Ensure that your school/club has maintained a good reputation

Tell your youngster how well they have done, win or lose

Help to take the goal nets down

Code of conduct for coaches/managers

Lead by example. Enjoy the occasion

Encourage your players to enjoy the match

Give positive comments and instructions during the match

Shake hands with the referee and opponents'
   coach/manager before and after the match

Display enthusiasm and good sportsmanship

Applaud both teams at the end of the match

Thank parents and spectators for their support

After cool-down praise the players for their effort,
   win or lose

YOU ARE WANTED

342. Junior clubs need you. Clubs need more like-minded, caring people to help out, take the strain off the coaching staff and make it enjoyable for everybody. The reward you will receive will not be in money but you will be rewarded by people who will recognise your hard work and dedication and who become your friends because of it. The value to youngsters cannot be calculated because your work is priceless. If clubs do not have enough volunteers they cannot keep going and if a club folds, there will inevitably be a negative effect on the community as a whole.

It is proven that youngsters are happier when they are active and entertained. They smile more, are fitter and healthier, and it keeps their brains and minds sharp and stimulated. If you volunteer at your local club, all of that is because of you and your colleagues. Long may it continue and congratulations to you for all your tremendous hard work.

STARTING A JUNIOR CLUB

343. Is there a need for a junior football club in your area – or do you believe that you can do better than the clubs that are currently operating? It is unlikely that you can run a club alone as they do tend to grow quickly from one team to several in a surprising short period of time. Your initial intentions will probably be to just start a team for your son and his friends, but once word gets around about the great job you're doing, more people will want to come onboard.

344. Once you have a number of committed parents and adult volunteers, you will need to look for suitable pitches and identify the rental costs for training and playing matches. By renting you will be provided with a ready made marked out pitch with goals and the pitch will be maintained and looked after for you. Next, you will need a football strip, footballs, bibs and cones for training.

Once you have all of this you need to put your costings together and decide how the club is going to be funded. Once you are up and running the children's weekly subscriptions can pay for the match referees and the running costs of the club.

345. Everyone is now bursting with enthusiasm and really looking forward to starting your matches. Do you have a team or club name yet? If not, have a competition and let the youngsters decide. Have you formed a committee to include the team manager and coach, a chairman, secretary and treasurer? You will now need to apply to a local league where you hope to take part in matches. Have a look at the standard first and go into one of the easier leagues as you will want your first season to go well. You might even gain promotion.

346. Do you have a squad of 16 players who are committed to the new team? It is a good idea to have a meeting with the parents to ensure their commitment and this also gives you an opportunity to go through your code of conduct and for them to sign it once it is agreed. Naturally you want everybody to enjoy the football experience and the time is now right to start training with the players and then to arrange some friendly matches.

347. Team bonding exercises are good to get the players having a laugh with each other. Playing another sport such as ten pin bowling is good to boost morale and involving all of the parents is even better – why not host a barbecue or even your very first fundraising social event. The rest is down to the team managers, committee and parents to ensure the youngsters have many years of fun growing up together. Good luck and enjoy the wonderful journey.

CHAPTER 9

Starting Your Own Football Academy

This is a great opportunity for you to have a full time job in football and become self-employed.

YOUR OWN FOOTBALL ACADEMY

348. In 1997 I recognised that in my home town there was a shortage of sporting activity for youngsters in the evenings. I asked several parents if their youngsters would like to attend a football academy. It was a resounding 'yes', but before I could start the most important thing was finding indoor facilities for six months of dark evenings, and then six months outside on grass in the light nights and good weather. As primary schools generally have no sports hall I contacted secondary schools in my area, and was fortunate enough to meet Jackson Sweeting who was Head of Sport at Haughton School in Darlington.

He was my last hope, as the other schools could not satisfy our needs. Jackson was brilliant and we agreed a rental that meant we not only had a gymnasium for the autumn and winter months but also a good grass surface to train upon in the spring and summer months. It was a fantastic feeling and I will always be indebted to Jackson.

Continuity is important as 'stop-start' does not work. Once a player starts training on a regular basis it becomes a way of life, their confidence grows and they start to meet new mates. If they only turn up occasionally they can feel themselves being left behind as regular attendees are improving at a faster rate, and they do not feel part of the new friendships which are being developed.

349. It was a great thing for the school to have us using their facilities. In addition to the new income they were receiving from us, the school's image was enhanced as every evening the local community witnessed happy children running enthusiastically around a football pitch enjoying their sport. It gave the school a real boost as they were seen to encourage after-school sporting activities, and this gave the school the confidence to open up further parts of the school to other activity groups. Everyone was a winner.

350. Okay, so now you have a base to work from. Your next task is to find players and this is easy. Write a letter to head teachers at your local primary and secondary schools and ask them if you can drop in flyers for them to distribute to the children in your target age groups. In this flyer you will need to give details of your history, qualifications and experience. You need to outline your objectives and then give a starting date with the cost of taking part. You will definitely need to have a CRB (Criminal Records Bureau) check which confirms that you are suitable to coach children.

351. I organise my groups as follows and it has worked well for 12 years.

Monday	Tuesday	Thursday	Friday
5–6 year olds 5–6pm	5–6pm	5–6pm	5–6pm
7–9 year olds 6–7pm	6–7pm	6–7pm	6–7pm
10–13 year olds 7–8pm	7–8pm	7–8pm	7–8pm

On Saturday mornings we coach 5–7 year olds from 9.30am to 11am and 8–10 year olds from 11am to 12.30pm.

In the evening groups we have a maximum of 24 players in each group, which fits the space perfectly and allows for six-a-side matches.

It's a good idea to try and put friends together in groups as it settles them in more quickly and usually guarantees good attendance.

352. Once you have a list of interested players to fit your evening or Saturday morning sessions, you need their details to set up a database on your computer. You need the name of the player, their address and telephone numbers, the child's date of birth, parents' names and any medical history and current medication and allergies.

353. If local schoolchildren do not fill all of the available spaces it's worth widening the net to include other schools and then putting an article or advertisement in the local press. Check the newspaper's circulation to see how many households it is going to, and make sure that the paper is being delivered to your target area.

354. With the starting date only a few weeks away you will need to start purchasing your football equipment. You will need to buy both indoor and outdoor footballs, four sets of different colour training bibs, flat cones for marking out lines and tall cones to be used for goals. These are the very basics you need to start your academy.

355. You have the details of the players and now you need to create a register for each individual training session. When the players and parents are at training they will pay your assistant the fee, and the player's name will be ticked off. You are now responsible for them.

It's a good idea to have a youngster who can greet the players and their families and build up a good ongoing relationship with them. In my case this helper was my son Michael, who was 14 when we started, and he helped me for five years. After taking each register, he assisted me with the training. If you limit your group to 24 players you will only need one person to assist you.

356. I was already a qualified coach with the English Football Coaches' Association and had eight years' experience as a professional player, junior team manager and as the father of a boy and girl. I knew how to build a positive, fun and disciplined environment where youngsters could enjoy their football.

I would recommend that a coach develops their skills by taking the FA coaching awards, which at grassroots level are quite easy to pass. This will give you the enthusiasm and encouragement to move on to the higher level courses. Your local county Football Association will provide a list of courses which will include Emergency First Aid and Child Welfare courses.

357. When you write to the child's parent confirming their place in the academy, include a copy of your rules and the code of conduct. The parents will be very impressed with your professionalism, especially if it is well typed on your academy's headed paper.

358. The children will now be bursting with enthusiasm to start. You can now start putting your training plans together. These sessions should start with a fun warm-up which could include a tag game or races between teams. All age groups love this type of initial movement.

Once the muscles are warm, stretching can take place

and it's a good idea to keep it simple and work on quads, groin stretching, calves and circular arm movements. This can be followed with a skill session where players have a ball each or a ball between two. A shooting session can follow, or a one-on-one dribbling session. Every player wants to play small-sided matches in training so use the last 30 minutes of each session to provide them with the opportunity to put their practised skills into match action.

If you have between 16 and 24 players a mini competition can take place where four teams can play each other in three ten-minute matches. These eagerly anticipated games are well received and players love to see which team has accumulated the most points.

359. This style of training session can be used for all ages from five-year-olds to adults. It involves movement, agility, co-ordination, balance, lots of individual time with the ball and learning technique and style to beat an opponent and score goals.

After the mini matches, stretches can end the session and a two-minute 'praising discussion' can take place where you confirm how well they have done while encouraging them to practise their skills at home.

Give them a big round of applause, award stickers to the best performers and hardest working players and tell them that you really look forward to seeing them at the next training session or match.

Making practise sharp, creating a learning environment and making it enjoyable will really stimulate a youngster's interest and make your academy an occasion that they would not want to miss.

360. Awarding stickers is a great additional way of rewarding good performance. We have stickers for best performance, most skilful player and good sportsmanship. Although the best performers will quite rightly receive the most stickers it's also a good idea to give a 'good attitude' award to players with less ability, who on every occasion work hard and give their very best. The 'most skilful' sticker is a good incentive for youngsters to practise at home and they love to put themselves forward for a sticker by showing me a new skill that they are trying to master. The sticker system works as it helps to keep them focused in the session and it keeps their attendance at a high level.

361. All the players at my academy, from five to 14 years old, receive an annual report which highlights their achievements and focuses on their strengths and areas where they can improve. These reports are complimentary to them, as the objective is to build their confidence and self esteem. Doing reports for 250 youngsters take a lot of time to complete, but it cements their relationship with my academy.

362. In July each year we have our annual presentation evening at which every player receives a trophy and a certificate to keep. In each of our three age groups there are awards for the players who have really excelled. These are: most dedicated player, best two-footed player, most skilful player, good attitude award, best newcomer, best passer, most improved player, best goalkeeper, personality of the year, most promising player, team player of the year and finally the player of the year.

363. Starting my own football academy is the my most accomplished achievement in my life, and that includes representing Manchester United and England and receiving the MBE from Prince Charles at Buckingham Palace.

It is not all about finding the next great professional player, but it is about encouraging thousands of youngsters to fall in love with this great game. It's about helping them to develop a mindset that will encourage them to live a healthy life and to encourage their family and friends to do the same. It is wonderful to see them grow and develop their own personalities and I love to hear of their achievements and events in their lives.

Most stories are happy ones of fun and joy, but you do hear of the downsides in their lives when mum and dad have had bad news regarding their jobs or their health. Some of my players' parents have tragically passed away. I feel that at the academy we have a responsibility to be there for both parents and children, giving them a stable boost with continued support.

Life is so precious. A lovely little boy, Darren Baker, trained with us for two years before tragically losing his life at just nine years old. Darren was diagnosed with pleurisy and a brain tumour and after a few weeks in hospital he passed away. Darren's parents, Sandra and Mike, and his sister Stacey were inspirational in the way that they dealt with the loss of their treasured son. Each year at our annual presentation evening we remember Darren when three players receive the Darren Baker Personality Award in memory of a wonderful lad.

364. It's important that the academy's administration is always accurate and carefully maintained. We give out regular letters to parents informing them of future events such as coaching courses in the school holidays. A dedicated academy bank account is important and as a self-employed person you will now be required to fill in an annual tax return. It is important that you record your monthly takings and retain all your receipts for outgoings. Make sure that you find out from the Inland Revenue what items you can and can not claim for.

CHAPTER 10

Football Fitness

A youngster with natural speed will always attract interest from sports teachers, coaches and football scouts as this gives them the base to work from to develop skills and technique. Quick players win football matches.

FOOTBALL FITNESS

365. When you think of football fitness you naturally look at the world's best players, and especially the attackers who score goals or the dynamic flair midfielders who run box-to-box to create goals.

The best teams have an abundance of players with speed, endurance, strength, agility, balance, co-ordination and minds fit enough to make quick decisions. If a player has these gifts and the ball skills, the desire, dedication and determination then bingo – this is one superb athlete and footballer!

366. As football has developed over the decades so have the football pitches, football boots and of course the football itself. Professional players must now work alongside sports dieticians to eat the correct food to give them the energy that is now required. Players are now aware of the importance of water and the need to eat the correct foods before and after a match.

367. Players with speed and skills will be wanted by every club so as a player it is an idea to streamline your running style by working with an athletic coach at your local harriers. I have witnessed players who have done this and their developed style looks so attractive to the eye. These players were made even quicker while also improving their balance at high speed.

368. Endurance can be improved by steadily increasing the distance that you run and how often you run. Young children like to run and play in short bursts, so generally running longer distances is not attractive to them. Children at nine years of age will start to run longer distances as they increase their lung capacity. Adults must monitor the child's endurance levels because pushing too hard can de-motivate them and in some cases cause a reluctance to take part. Very gradual improvement with huge praise will see the desired effect.

369. With the correct food, children should be left to grow naturally and should not be allowed to use weights until they are at least 16 years old. Even then it should only be light weights. Strength training will help prevent injury, providing that it is used correctly.

Take Andy Murray, the British tennis player, as an example. He moved to a level of tennis where he was in the world's top 20 players, and then found that breaking into the top 10 was a struggle. He changed coach and this move gave him the impetus to work on what was required to compete with the top players. His actual ability with the racket was unquestioned but there were doubts about his strength and stamina compared with the very best players in the world.

Working with a fitness coach, he trained very hard off the court and as his strength and stamina improved so did his results. Instead of fading in the latter sets of a match he was able to 'hang in there' and this gave him the encouragement to step up his strength and physical work to an even higher level. Mentally he knew he was now in good physical shape and in 2008 he reached his first Grand Slam Final. Once again he saw what could be achieved with this new body and he then went on a run of tournament wins, beating Roger Federer four times in succession and beating new world No 1 Rafael Nadal.

I have seen this happen to footballers when they have particularly worked on developing upper body strength. However, be careful when developing leg muscles using weights as you can become cumbersome and lose agility and your natural skills can suffer.

370. All top footballers, athletes and sportspeople have solid core muscles which are in the abdominal and lower back areas. These muscles play an important role in controlling posture and balance. Strong abdominal and back muscles provide the foundation to improve fitness and athletic performance. The abdominal muscles are the foundation on which all explosive movements are based. These muscles are the centre of your power base and developing this key area will provide you with the power to improve the effectiveness of your physical actions. Doing sit-ups every day is a basic start to giving you strength and power which will give you the confidence that will improve to football performance. Believe me it works and it will boost your mental strength knowing you are stronger than anybody else on the pitch.

371. The first five to ten yards in football are very important – please remember this. Explosive sprinting over the first few yards will probably put you in front of everybody else. Quick arm movement will also help with the acceleration, as does taking short, sharp steps. Again working with a coach at your local athletics club can make a big difference.

372. Research has shown that in a 90-minute match players are either walking or jogging for half of the match. Yes, 50% of the time the players are hardly moving. For 30 minutes, or a third of the match, they are running at average speed and they are only running or sprinting 10% of the time. So while you do need to have all-round athletic ability the real difference is your speed over a short running distance – being there first.

373. In the eyes of children it is brilliant when they turn up to training and see the goals, cones, and footballs laid out ready to start. Add to this different colours of training equipment and it all looks even more attractive. Children love to take part in obstacle-style activities, which makes them use their minds to find the best ways to achieve the skill. At my academy we use red poles for them to run in and out of, yellow hurdles for them to jump over and coloured marker cones for them to stride over or step to in side-to-side movements. I also use green hoops which the players have to navigate through using high knees. Put all these together in an obstacle course, make it competitive and you will have youngsters from five years old to 19 years old asking you to set this activity up more often. It's a really enjoyable warm-up session, and the participants are using agility, co-ordination, balance and varied jumping movements while building up their endurance.

MOVEMENT: FLEXIBILITY

374. Incredibly, from the age of 10–12 years old a child starts to lose their suppleness and flexibility because their muscles start to increase in size and strength. Make football activities fun and start at an early age with stretching and flexibility exercises. Stretching provides the joints with a greater range of movement and therefore helps sporting performance.

A stretching cool-down after football and sporting activity is just as important as the warm-up as is helps relieve muscle and joint stiffness.

Tell the children that they are doing the same stretches as the world's top footballers. This activity will encourage children to make this activity part of their everyday life to make them feel good. Many elite footballers now use yoga and Pilates as part of their flexibility programme.

MOVEMENT: CO-ORDINATION

375. Co-ordination is the ability to action a range of movements smoothly and accurately. Nearly one in ten children has co-ordination difficulties; however, with regular football skill sessions, these problems can be solved to ensure that previously difficult movements are streamlined to produce a smooth and stylish performance. Repetition and practise using football skills with the feet and also rugby and basketball passing movements with the hands will see a positive improvement.

MOVEMENT: BALANCE

376. Look at the great dribbling footballers, or the speedy rugby winners; they have the balance skills to run with the ball at speed and can weave inside and outside of opponents at speed while maintaining their balance even after aggressive tackles. This style of player generally has two equally effective feet and side-to-side movement at speed comes naturally to them. Copying the movements of downhill skiers as they weave in and out of training poles and cones and jumping over hurdles will lead to an improvement if used on a regular basis. Also, watch the amazing gymnasts as they do somersaults on the six-inch-wide bar; now that balancing act does take years of dedicated practise! Balance is the base to develop your athletic technique.

MOVEMENT: AGILITY

377. At the world famous dog show Crufts, have you seen the dogs in the agility classes perform? They have the agility and skills to change direction at speed. Dribbling footballers, downhill skiers or rugby wingers can change direction effortlessly in a smooth, efficient way while still remaining well balanced.

If you can improve your agility and combine this skill with improving flexibility, co-ordination and balance while moving quickly with a football then you will be thrilled with the result. Dedication to practise and repetition will reap the rewards for you. This is one of the key areas for players to focus on to improve their football. Agility can be taught – with practise.

MOVEMENT: QUICKNESS/SPEED

378. If you were to ask any coach, from a junior football team to a professional football team, they would say that this skill is probably the biggest attribute they would want their players to have. They would certainly say speed and ability. Speed is a skill. And what a skill it is when used to its maximum effect.

Speed is natural; you are either born a naturally speedy athlete or not. Can you improve your speed? The answer is yes, but only a little. There are two types of speed and quickness: one is in movement and the other is a quick mind to make speedy decisions on the pitch.

The best way to improve speed is by improving your running style and practising moving in and out of cones and poles in a Ryan Giggs style of balanced zig-zag movements.

If you are a little heavy, losing a few pounds will help you improve, as will agility and aerobic work in the gym. Playing one- or two-touch football in training games will certainly aid your decision-making in matches.

I have noticed that players who wear spectacles off the pitch are a little bit slower on the pitch to control the ball and then look for a player to pass to. It could only be a fraction of a second but that could be the difference from being an average player to being an excellent player.

A coach could think that these are slow-thinking players but it is actually the time it takes to refocus for a glasses-wearing player. The best way to help this type of player is contact lenses for football and sport. I would not recommend this for children, but perhaps for teenagers upwards. It will take several weeks for them to get used to putting these foreign objects in their eyes but once they are used to wearing them they will see a big improvement in their quicker decision making. Fractions of a second in sport can make a huge difference.

MOVEMENT: ENDURANCE AND STAMINA

379. You might be quick, which a fantastic attribute to have, but are you fit enough to use that quickness right up until the last seconds of a match. It would be a shame if your team needed a goal in the last minute of the match and they needed one last quick surge of quickness from you. A through ball was slotted through the oppositions defence and you as quickest player on the pitch can see yourself sprinting through to drill home the match winning goal and be the goal hero. However your legs were heavy, your energy was shot and the opportunity for glory was gone. If only you had worked harder to develop your stamina.

380. At professional clubs, pre-season training is seen as the most important time to build up endurance and stamina. The players have come back from a two-month rest and they are weighed to see if they have put on any extra pounds. Some clubs actually fine players who have put on weight during the holidays. The first two weeks of pre-season training includes focused stamina work, where some clubs go and work with Army fitness instructors or take players to the beach and have them running up and down the sand dunes or doing timed runs on the athletics track. Most professional clubs work in the mornings and afternoons at this time of the season, and sessions could include endurance work and time in the gym in the morning and then ball work in the afternoon.

Usually after these extremely demanding exertions are complete, two to three friendly matches per week are arranged. Some clubs like to play weaker opposition as they give the players the opportunity to build confidence and practise set plays and score some goals.

381. Some people can naturally and effortlessly run for miles. In football you see box-to-box midfielders who are hardly blowing at the end of the match. Obviously goals can be scored at any time in a match, but if you or your team-mates don't have the stamina to compete for the full duration of the match then you are vulnerable to late goals being scored against you. If you look at a record of when you have conceded goals in matches, you will see whether you have any weak periods of time. Fatigue causes muscles to tighten up, agility and co-ordination to fade and reactions to become slower.

I call natural athletes 'Duracell' players, named after the batteries which the manufacturers say can go on for longer than others. How they do it? In most cases it is natural and they were born with this skill. They tend to be one-pace plodders; however if they are also naturally quick then you have a fantastic base to work on. This type of hardworking player tends to be leaner and less muscular than the quick sprinters.

Generally young children do not like running or even walking long distances, but it's possible to improve distance running from the age of nine, when their lung capacity improves. Just do this very gradually and write down how far they ran, how long it took, how the player felt and how long it took them to recover. You do not want to put off a young player, though, so give them a distance that they can run and be successful and happy with.

While they are involved with this extra running they must eat and drink correctly before and after the action as they are using extra energy. The most important part is that their water intake is good to stop dehydration. Youngsters who are tired are more likely to have injuries than fitter players with more stamina and endurance.

FOOTBALL INJURIES AND ILLNESS

You will know your children well enough to know when something is wrong and they are not firing on all cylinders. With immediate effect do not risk further injury or illness. Taking part in sporting activity will not help their recovery, will not help them to play well and will not help their team. Rest and recovery will boost their energy levels and once they are rejuvenated they will return with even more enthusiasm.

382. The majority of football injuries can be solved by prevention. The major causes of injuries are doing too much training or playing too many matches over a short period of time and an ignorance of the importance of warming up before the activity and cooling down afterwards. It is the early and teenage growing years, when the body shows particular growth, where injuries can occur. Parents and coaches should be aware of each youngster's sporting capabilities and they need to watch them very carefully and monitor the intensity of the activity.

A good footballer will no doubt have other sporting skills and they will be offered training and matches at different clubs doing different sports. A talented sportsman can end up training and playing matches seven days a week and not only will this dull his energy but it will also make him vulnerable to injuries. You could also witness tired, lethargic players with weakening enthusiasm.

383. Always ensure that the players' muscles are warm before they attempt stretches. Gentle jogging to start with, followed by mid-speed turns, squats, jumps and side-to-side stepping will warm up the key muscle groups, which are quadriceps, calves, groin and hamstrings. Once stretches are complete, higher speed jogging followed by quicker runs with a change of direction can take place.

I see youngsters at school and junior football clubs run out onto the pitch and with no warm-up start shooting at goal – either with one ball or with other teams all shooting footballs at the same time at the poor goalkeeper. A good warm-up will reflect positively on the school or junior club and the players will feel confident in the knowledge that their health is being looked after and that they are now ready to start the activity with their bodies fit for action.

384. Sometimes, adults expect gifted youngsters to perform well all of the time but in reality it is not always possible. It is fantastic to see the tremendous enthusiasm that young footballers display, and we do not want to dent this energy, but we must protect them.

OVERUSE INJURIES AND ILLNESS

385. If players, parents and coaches are aware of potential injuries then they can prevent the injury happening in the first place. An overworked and overtired player will be obvious to spot as their whole body language will be different and their enthusiasm and sparkle is reduced. A short break from sporting activity, more sleep and perhaps a massage can quickly return the player to their previous energetic and enthusiastic state.

386. Overuse or overplaying can cause a number of problems where the muscles, ligaments and tendons can develop at a quicker rate than the skeleton of the youngsters. Doing too much activity can cause injury to the attachments to the muscle or tendons to the bone.

387. There are two injuries that I have come across in youngsters. One is called Osgood Schlatters Disease and the other one is Severs Disease.

Osgood Schlatters is common in youngsters up to 16 years old with the main symptom of pain just below the kneecap, where you might find a small bump. It is usually worse during and after activity. This bump is permanent although in time it becomes painless. It tends to ease with rest, but the pain can last for a few months or until the player has stopped growing. This condition happens for no apparent reason but it does appear more often in growing players who are also taking part in too much physical activity. The condition is not serious and is likely to go after a rest period. Treatment is not usually given, however if the condition last for a two year period an operation might be required.

Light sporting can continue but may make the condition worse. A complete break from sport might be required if the pain increases.

388. Severs Disease can effect children from the ages of ten and 13 years of age. A pain can be felt in the heels while taking part in sport. It is caused by the growth of the bone taking place at a faster rate than the tendons. It can be exacerbated by overuse. Running and playing sport on hard surfaces increases the risk of getting this injury. The best treatment is rest and a reduction of the intense sporting activity. If the condition persists after rest, and medication does not reduce the inflammation, a cast might need to be worn for up to six weeks to give the injury a chance to recover. The condition will start to improve when the two growth areas join – usually around the age of 16.

389. Overuse injuries account for half of injuries at secondary school age. Players who return after injury can return too soon and they can make the original injury much worse if they are not monitored. Early return can also put stress and pressure on other parts of the body and cause new injury problems. Highly motivated youngsters who love to play many sports are most at risk to over activity.

390. In football the most common injuries are bruising, cuts and scrapes anywhere on the body, and strains and pulls on the calf, groin and hamstring areas. More serious injuries are breaks to the ankles, legs, hands and arms and ligament damage to the knees and ankles. Head injuries do occur with players colliding heads causing bumps and bruises. Obviously all injuries have a different severity and in a fast moving contact sport, injuries are part and parcel of the game.

With youngsters a simple knock can be put right very quickly by giving them assurance that in one minute the pain will have gone and they will be playing again. They look to you to give them the confidence and assurance that everything is going to be okay. Distracting them by talking about their favourite team or player will take their mind off the injury. You do build up an idea of how each player reacts to knocks and bumps and this history does help you deal with each individual player.

391. In a couple of minutes you can assess if the player is able to continue the training session or the match. Obviously with a strain or ligament injury it is best to rest the player from the activity. With a potential break it is important that the player receives hospital treatment, with an x-ray or scan determining the problem area and the level of the problem. With a serious injury it is important that the player is taken to hospital immediately.

All key people at matches should have their mobile phones at the ready, with fully charged batteries, in case they need to call the emergency services and the family of any injured players. The management should always carry a well-stocked first aid kit and the names and contact telephone numbers of the youngsters' parents. They should also know if the youngster is on any medication and what it is. Also ensure that people only apply the first aid that they are trained for. The medical welfare of the player comes well before the result of the match, no matter how good a player is and how much the team is going to miss his ability.

392. Asthma symptoms are coughing, wheezing, shortness of breath and a tightness in the chest. The quickest way of dealing with it is to make an appointment with your GP and have the asthma confirmed. The doctor will tell you that asthma occurs when the airways are inflamed and become narrow, making it difficult to breathe in and out normally. The doctor will access the level of asthma you have and depending on this they will either confirm that you can continue playing football or suggest that you do not.

If the doctor gives a youngster the go-ahead to continue, he will prescribe an inhaler which they will recommend you to use before and after exercise to prevent the symptoms returning.

393. Asthma sufferers need regular exercise as it improves their breathing and general fitness. Youngsters with asthma who do not take exercise can develop breathing problems and being overweight can make the problem more serious.

Parents must make coaches are aware of children with any health issues and parents must ensure that the asthma sufferer always has their own prescribed inhaler with them and that they know how and when to use it. Never use somebody else's inhaler.

394. We do have diabetic young players and they tend to be well educated on their condition and know what action to take and when. They know that before during and after training and matches that they need to check their blood sugar levels and that they could need a small snack break.

Type 1 diabetics are okay to participate in football as this exercise is very important to assist their overall health. Parents and coaches must be aware of the needs of both asthma and diabetes sufferers.

395. Growth spurt injuries from 12–15 years old can cause both physical and mental problems as youngsters are growing into their own bodies and not knowing what to expect. Their energy levels can fall, their bones grow faster than the soft tissues and they start to lose flexibility. During this period of their lives they are mentally in no man's land between being a child and a young adult and parents, teachers and coaches can play a huge part in helping them understand and come to terms with these changes.

During the growth spurt, players are more vulnerable to injury, they can seem ungainly, and their co-ordination, balance, agility and strength can be affected. It is a phase where they need time to get to know their new body and their more adult and macho attitude. It is up to their parents to guide them through the activities that they take part in and to monitor their training and match schedule.

The cool down is as important as the warm up as this helps stop muscles tightening up and it also assists in clearing waste products from muscles.

396. After an injury, do not push a youngster back into training too early. Instead, ensure they rest and recover. As it is difficult to watch your very enthusiastic football-loving youngster for 24 hours a day, it is a good idea to give a letter to their sports teacher or junior club coach outlining the injury and asking that they do not take part in any sporting activity until the injury has healed. At school they can still go mad in the playground at breaktime so stop that as well. You do not want to hold them back and quell their enthusiasm, but this is for their own good.

397. In an overworked player you will see the following characteristics: swelling in the problem area; painful when touched; discomfort, aching legs; and stiffness; visible swelling; negative body language; tired and disappointed; not the usually bouncy enthusiasm.

Before this situation arises, take the player out of all sporting activities and give them a good rest to revive both their body and their enthusiasm. Without adequate rest the problems will not go away.

CHAPTER 11

Referees

WHY BE A REF?

398. People start refereeing at different ages and for different reasons. A young person moving from junior football to adult football may feel that their physical strengths and footballing ability will not be good enough for them to get into a senior team. Some adults have enjoyed their lives playing in a team but have received an injury, or have had to retire from team football, or have decided that they cannot afford to risk injury. Either way, they do not want to give up participating in football.

The best way to become qualified is to contact your local refereeing co-ordinator – you can get this information from your county Football Association. You will need a CRB check and you will go on a course to achieve a qualification. Believe me once you have qualified your phone will not stop ringing, and there are some good match fees to earn.

399. It's the toughest job in football, no doubt. You give a decision and one lot of players and supporters are happy that you got it right on their behalf, but the opposition players and supporters believe you are the dizziest person on the planet. Sixty seconds later you give a decision the other way and the other team's supporters now believe that you're the dizziest person on the planet! Do not go into refereeing and expect to please people all of the time.

400. Can a referee ever win? The answer is yes – if a referee has the drive and ambition of a player he can gain promotion through the leagues and become a professional referee. If a referee shows a lot of common sense, shows that he is enjoying the match, knows the rules inside out, is physically fit, is calm and can talk to players in a friendly but positive manner then yes, he can win. Oh yes, nearly forgot: he also needs good eyesight!

401. Ask any player at any level and they will say that the best referees are the ones where you hardly know they are on the pitch. This style of referee lets the players be the stars on the pitch. Spectators come to watch the players perform and not to see the referee perform. Referees of children's under-10 small-sided matches do a great job. They let the youngsters play, give them bags of individual praise and even give them a demonstration if they make a foul throw. They keep the rules relaxed and the atmosphere happy. Referees at this age group will also have a quiet word in a coach's, parent's or spectator's ear if they believe the adult has stepped over the 'loudness' mark.

SUPPORT THE REF

402. If adults are seen to respect the referee, then even the youngest starters will copy and will grow up to respect the referee. If the opposite happens, a player and his parents and coach can spend too much time looking for the referee to make a mistake and miss the great things happening in the game. I say to the players that are continually appealing to the match officials that they are losing at least 10% of their effectiveness and enjoyment, as their focus and concentration is not on achieving something positive in the match. Leave the referee alone and get on with the task of having fun.

403. Of course referees are honest and give the decisions that their eyes see. They can only give a decision on what they see and in a fast-moving game it is not always possible to be in the correct position to see an incident that happens in a split second. In junior and amateur football the referee sometimes has to guess a decision as he does not have the advantage of having assistants. Even if there is a volunteer linesman in an amateur match, the referee will only accept ball in and out of play decisions from them.

MEDIA INFLUENCE

404. After the players, the referees are the most important people in junior football. Why? Because if we do not have them we do not play football matches.

Professional football is now seen live on TV around the planet. Perhaps 200 million people can see a live game and see players making mistakes, which fans understand is part of the game. What fans are not as tolerant about is when the referee and his assistants make errors of judgment. Their decisions have to be made in a split second, when there are 22 players on the field playing a game at high speed, with a number of players trying to cheat to deceive the referee.

What exaggerates the match officials' mistakes is the comments from the TV 'experts' in their lovely warm studios showing us the ref's errors in slow motion from 10 different camera angles.

The assistant referee or linesman is also seen to be running up and down the touchline while behind him 20,000 biased fans are telling him how useless he is.

At half-time and full time, questionable decisions are debated in the TV studios and then the losing coach is told that the ref has made a mistake and asked what he thinks about it. Well he certainly is not going to say he is happy about it, and sometimes coaches use the ref's errors as an excuse to deflect attention away from their own team's poor performance. Unfortunately the professional game can have a negative knock-on effect in junior and amateur football, where the players copy the disrespect shown by professional players.

405. Because of the huge TV coverage of high profile matches, supporters see that match officials are being criticised and they believe that it's normal and okay to question the referee's honesty and decision making. This filters down to junior football and amateur adult football, where the referee's job is even harder as he often doesn't have an assistant ref or linesman to help him. The poor ref now has to give offside decisions and watch all of the players all of the time. He needs eyes in the back of his head to function properly.

Children see parents and spectators questioning decisions and they see it as okay to join in. The question is then asked: 'Why is there a shortage of referees?' The probable answer is that while referees want to enjoy the sport and exercise, they are sick of the constant aggravation from the players and from the touchline and so they give up on officiating.

CHANGING THE RULES

406. How can we solve this problem and attract more young referees into the game? Firstly the governing bodies of football should protect referees and give them stricter rules. Nobody dares to argue with a match official in rugby as they know they will be severely dealt with.

This is what I think should happen. If a referee gives a free kick in football and it is questioned, they should move the free kick closer to the complaining team's own goal. If that means it ends up in the penalty area, give a penalty kick against them. If verbal criticism continues in a match, referees should have the power to send a player to the sin bin for 10 minutes as they do in rugby and ice hockey. If teams accumulate too many bookings and sendings off, leagues should deduct points from them during the season.

By making these rule changes, referees would be given more support from the governing bodies. Verbal aggression on the pitch would calm down as teams would lose the immediate advantage due to their players' inappropriate behaviour. These new rules would also add a little bit more spice to the match day experience for supporters.

407. As part of a coach's development, coaches of all levels should have to take an exam which would involve them refereeing two matches: one for children and another match for adults. They would not be allowed the 'luxury' of assistant referees. They would be videoed and they could then see a playback of their performance. They would be asked for their views and they would be sit an examination on the Laws of the Game.

TV football commentators would also be asked to take part in these examinations. The doubters would then see how difficult a referee's job is.

PLAYER/REFEREE RELATIONSHIP

408. When I was a professional player, you could always have a conversation with a referee during the game. He would compliment you on a good piece of skill. If you were to tell him he was having a bad game and making poor decisions, he would tell you that you weren't having the best of games yourself. The banter was good and it made the referee/player relationship fun. I was playing in a match at Chelsea once when I mistimed a tackle near the touchline in front of the main stand and fouled a Chelsea player. The crowd went crazy and wanted me booked or sent off. It was a foul, I agree, and the crowd thought that the referee was giving me a real lecture. Actually he was from my part of the country and was recommending a restaurant that he thought I should try! His final words to me were 'Steady with the tackling, Paul'.

I think it would be fantastic for professional referees to have a small microphone so that we could hear their conversations with their assistants and even hear them talk to the players, as long as this was vetted by the TV producer.

VIDEO TECHNOLOGY

409. Will video technology come into the game as it does in tennis and cricket? I am sure it will. It adds to the enjoyment in those sports when you look to see whether the batsman was in or out or whether the tennis ball was in or out. It does add to the drama, no doubt. If the ref in big matches was unsure about the ball crossing the goal line he could call for the fourth official's opinion and within seconds he would be given the result. I do hope that video technology is only used in the future for goal/no goal decisions, however, as we don't want football to become a stop-start affair.

CHAPTER 12

Professional Football Academies

'Show me a person who is not passionate about their
profession and I will soon show you someone who
has failed.'

HOW DO THEY WORK?

410. Always keep in mind that these football academies or
centres of excellence are businesses. Each time the
footballers who attend these academies go for training, they
are going into an organised business set up. The ultimate
aim of a football academy or a centre of excellence is quite
simple. They have to produce players who will eventually
play in the first team and financially they need to develop
players that they can sell at a substantial profit.

411. Over 97% of youngsters who are invited to a
professional football club's academy or centre of excellence
do not play for that club's first team. A lot of first team

managers take little interest in their club's youth development as they believe that they will not be at that club long enough to see the youngsters come through the system and challenge for a first team place. Less than 1% of 8–10-year-olds who train at a professional club continue in professional football.

412. Initially it is a great compliment for the youngsters and their parents to be asked to go for trials at a club, especially when they are asked to sign a contract. This is a very competitive industry and clubs are scared that the next superstar could slip from their grasp and be signed by their nearest rival. As this would be embarrassing to a club's scouting and recruitment department, clubs will trial hundreds of players who show a level of football talent and then sign the ones that they believe they can develop into a professional player. They turn over hundreds of players but only the very best will stay, and they will only stay while they are performing on a consistent basis. To put it bluntly: if they fail to perform they will be replaced.

413. Academies are costly operations to run; therefore they will be monitored by the club to see whether they produce players for the first team or players that the club can sell for a healthy profit. The quality of the coaches and their skills in motivating and developing youngsters will also be monitored and they will be encouraged to further improve their coaching qualifications.

A coach at an academy or a centre of excellence would require the UEFA B qualification while working towards the UEFA A standard. Some clubs will allow a coach to follow a team through the age groups, while others will ask the coach to stay with an age group for a longer period of time. Due to finances some clubs have had to do away with their academies and some smaller professional clubs have even had to get rid of their reserve team to save money.

414. Once signed, players in all age groups from eight-year-olds to 19-year-olds will train two to three evenings each week. The parents and players could be in the car for two hours going to and from training, and on a Saturday or a Sunday an away match can be played against other academy or centre of excellence teams with a round trip journey of four to five hours. This is a heavy commitment for families to make, especially when so many players will be released and so few will last long enough to become a professional player.

During this period with a club they expect the players and parents to be totally dedicated to them; however, at any time they can dismiss your youngster without any further help to further their football opportunities elsewhere.

415. As a caring and loving parent you naturally want the best for your young ones and you will support them through thick and thin. Be aware that clubs obviously have some players who are more gifted than others and they will want these special players to play matches to further develop their talent. Clubs need squads to play matches in each of their age groups and they will pad teams out with players who have no chance of being a professional player but who will make a team up to give the special players a platform to improve.

If you feel that your youngster is being used as a 'make the numbers up' player, it is worth speaking to the academy or centre of excellence director to find out the club's true opinion of your youngster. Knowing this information could save you years of wasted time, energy and travel costs and it could return the player to an environment where he can enjoy his football with his team-mates in a junior team. He could then return to being the 'big fish' in the junior team and this could then boost his confidence and improve his football at a less demanding level. It could well save you travelling long distances two to three times a week to the training centre, or long away trips at the weekend.

416. Clubs do have regular reviews with parents where a two-way conversation can take place. Generally clubs do not want to get into discussions with parents on a weekly or monthly basis. They want to coach the players on an evening and play the matches on a weekend without parental interference. However, at the review meeting you can put forward any questions you have. This can be a nervous time for players and parents wondering if their youngster is being 'kept on'. By asking the correct questions you can find out how they rate your child and his potential. It is important that their school work is not being affected and that you are happy with the coaching that they are receiving.

417. I have seen parents who are so excited that their boy has been offered a trial that they believe that he is on the road to stardom. They have almost taken it for granted that he will be wearing the first team shirt and they even believe that the full international jersey will follow along soon after. They openly boast to their friends and work colleagues and this can cause some jealousy which could be avoided.

It is important to remain modest and understand that if Junior receives a trial, or a contract or a scholarship, they have done very well, but they do not want you putting further pressure on them to perform. Be modest and explain to your family, friends and colleagues that your son has been invited to a trial or to sign a contract, but that the road is long and a lot of hard work is required to stay involved with the club. Congratulate your lad on his invitation and explain that you are proud of him and that you want him to enjoy the coaching and the experience. Tell him to continue to give his best, make new friends and show the coaches that he has a positive attitude to learn.

SCOUT'S CHECKLIST

'It is still skill and creativity that makes the difference between winners and losers.'

STEVE HIGHWAY, LIVERPOOL FC ACADEMY DIRECTOR

418. Most professional clubs have local, area and regional scouts who watch school teams, junior clubs and district teams looking for 'the special one'. The good scouts develop a good knowledge of their area and will know the teams to watch in each age group. They have a checklist to work to which will include the following.

Do the players on view:

Have speed and acceleration and a good strong physique?

Have an athletic appearance and style?

Show a coolness and composure on the ball and good overall technique?

Have good first-touch control using both feet, thighs, chest and head?

Have a positive style, confidence and enthusiasm to want the ball?

Pass the ball accurately and quickly over a variety of distances with both feet?

Show intelligence in their passing while not giving the ball away?

Have an understanding of their position?

Have a high work rate, showing good stamina and leadership qualities to motivate team-mates?

Have a determination to tackle hard to win the ball?

Make consistent and quick decisions i.e. when to pass the ball, run and dribble with it or cross and shoot?

Show good vision and see team-mates in good positions?

Make quick decisions?

Want the ball when they are winning and losing?

Have mental strength and concentration?

Have the respect of their team-mates and a positive outlook?

Have a drive to achieve and be successful?
Show a 'never give in' mentality?

'When the going gets tough, the tough get going.'

Players can have all the abilities in the world but without mental toughness their abilities will not shine through. If a player had all of these strengths he would probably be the best footballer ever created. If a scout is happy that a player has a number of these attributes, then he will be happy to put the player's name forward for a trial.

'Trust is the emotional glue that holds every team together. In times of trial, it transforms a group of committed individuals into a team of individuals committed to each other.'

419. A trialist can attend trials at a football academy or a centre of excellence for up to six weeks. The club must give written notice to the child's junior club informing them that they are taking the player on trial. Clubs can take players up to under 12 years of age within one hour's travel of the club and the rule is 90 minutes' maximum travel for 13- to 16-year-olds. Players can only trial at one club at a time. From the age of nine, players can sign schoolboy forms which are renewable every one or two years.

When a player is 16 they can join a club's youth training scheme or if they have done particularly well they could be offered a scholarship which can last for a maximum of three years. Officially you can sign a professional contract at 17 years old.

Players are expected to continue their education. There are various courses at A level, BTEC and GNVQ level.

At under-9s, under-10s and under-11s they play eight-a-side and then 11-a-side after that.

420. During the trial period the player requires settling in time. The surroundings are unfamiliar, the coach and players are new, and you are not sure how your abilities compare with your training colleagues. How long have the other players been training with the club and will they even pass to you? It will take a few sessions to understand the coach's requirements and to get used to the pace of the movement and the passing. The players' strengths and weaknesses are unknown to you as yours are to them. The artificial surface could be new to you and could be slower or faster than you are used to. Go to enjoy yourself, try to relax and do the simple things well. Do not try skills that are foreign to you but do the things that you are good at. Once the coach gives you praise and the other players see your ability you will all start to feel relaxed with each other. The coach should have the experience to allow you a number of sessions to settle in before judging you. Sometimes a player can have fantastic talent but may not develop if they are in the wrong environment; however a player with lesser ability could surprise you in the right environment. The correct environment and atmosphere is everything.

421. Clubs can look for different skill requirements in a player and this can vary from country to country. Countries like Brazil believe that if the player plays with freedom and his skills and technique are mastered, winning games will come as a consequence. A lot of the successful Brazilian players come from difficult backgrounds where there is not a lot of money. They played outside for hours with their friends and they did not receive organised coaching until they were 16 years old. In Brazil they say that coaching children at a young age can limit their creativity with the ball, so the ten million Brazilian kids are given many opportunities to play unstructured football. With young players they ask 'How did you play?' rather than 'Did you win?'

422. One of the things scouts and coaches look for in a youngster is the size of his parents. This gives them a guide as to the possible height and build of the player. If they see a tiny player and their parents are a similar build they know it is unlikely he is going to grow into a towering central defender, so they can develop the style of the player to suit a particular position. There are not many tiny players in professional football so the ones that are selected have to be exceptional.

423. Date of birth should be considered when players are trialling or being judged at clubs. A player of, say, ten years old born in September could have quite an advantage in terms of physical and mental maturity over a player of nine born in July the following year. A coach or scout could look at a group of players without knowing their dates of birth and could say that one player is struggling, but he is in fact 10 months younger than the other players and could dismiss this lad's chance of staying on. In the next 10 months, when the player has grown, he could be the best player in the group. A number of people dismissed George Best as a child saying he was too small and too skinny; how wrong they were.

424. The historical background of the youngster also needs to be taken into consideration as clubs could miss a real gem. A quiet little kid who is an introvert and who lives in a small village in the countryside could initially take it badly when he trains and plays with and against more outgoing, more streetwise youngsters. Also, a player with no brothers or sisters might not be as robust as a player who has two brothers who have, let's say, had 'competitive' matches between themselves. If this type of player has the hunger and the ability he will gradually get used to the environment, grow into it and feel comfortable.

425. It's good to feel nervous before a match as it provides the motivation required to give you the drive and the energy to focus on the objective. A bit of nervous energy helps you rise to the challenge. With experience you will find your fear level and channel this experience into positive energetic activity. Often when someone says 'You can't do that' it can really motivate a player into facing their fears and trying to prove them wrong.

426. Be the most dedicated player in your group and do not be embarrassed to believe it. I say to players I represent that it is in their power to accomplish their dreams. It is up to the player how much work, effort and dedication they are prepared to put in to achieve their ultimate goal.

Their attitude must be 100% focused at all times. Their effort must be total. They have to be the first on the training ground and the last off it. They must support the manager in every decision he makes and they must give praise to their team-mates at all times. Work hard for the manager and he will give you opportunities. Work hard for your team, have a 'never say die' attitude, and be fit enough to cover every blade of grass in matches to achieve the win.

'A true leader has the confidence to stand alone, the courage to make tough decisions, and the compassion to listen to the needs of others. He does not set out to be a leader, but becomes one by the quality of his action and the integrity of his intent. In the end, leaders are much like eagles…they don't flock, you find them one at a time.'

427. It is difficult to judge a player on one performance. Anybody who does this is being unfair to the player and should know better. If you saw a player for the first time, you might be disappointed, but then in the next two matches he could be fantastic. If I was going to sign a player I would want to see him in at least two home games and two away games.

428. In an adult match of 90 minutes a player is only in contact with the ball for a little over two minutes. In children's football on a big pitch they play 11-a-side and only play 50 minutes in total so they are touching the ball for less than two minutes each. It's what the player does without the ball for the majority of time that might catch the scout's or coach's eye.

429. Examples of the attributes that clubs are looking for in a player are: skill, intelligence, speed, composure under pressure, game intelligence, attitude, personality, strength, balance, mobility, agility, endurance, self belief, a competitive edge and a winning mentality.

430. In England there are over 5,000 youngsters training each week at Premier League and Football League clubs. The role of the academy or centre of excellence director is to create elite athletes for his club. Less than 1% of 8–10 year olds training at professional clubs will make it as a professional player with that club.

431. As a youngster I captained my school in a number of sports and played for my county at both football at rugby. I was the kicker and top points scorer for the county at rugby until the day came when both county football and rugby teams had a match on the same Saturday. It was very unfortunate as I had been totally committed to both sports and the dates had not clashed before. My love for football was way higher than my love for rugby and I had been invited to join Manchester

United, Leeds United, Newcastle United and a number of other clubs.

My father explained my dilemma to my county rugby coach, stating the unfortunate clash of matches, but the coach was adamant that if I chose to play in the county football match I would not be selected to play for the rugby team again.

Manchester United could have questioned my love of football if I had missed the football match so I played for the county football team. Sadly it was not my fault but I was not selected to play county rugby again. I had been tipped for international rugby honours but a few years later I was grateful to receive the call-up for the England youth football squad.

432. As a player develops and matures at a professional football club, the winning mentality becomes more important. It makes financial sense for a club to develop their own youngsters instead of spending high transfer fees. Also local players are more committed to their local team, especially if they supported this team as a youngster. Winning at professional first team level is everything; second is nowhere. That's what the mentality was when I was at Manchester United and it has not changed. At any age professional clubs will look to see if the player has that little bit of an edge to win games. They will look to see his reaction to winning and losing. The coach will not be disappointed if the player shows early signs of being angry in defeat or is not happy with his own performance or even that of his team-mates. It is not a good sign if a player in any age group looks happy after a defeat, especially when he and his team-mates have not performed well.

433. Coaches will also see how the player reacts after a win. Showing respect by shaking hands with an opponent after a game is correct, but celebrating with great enthusiasm in the privacy of your changing room with your team-mates is fantastic and shows what winning means to you. The top professional footballers, with great financial riches, have a number of things in common but the biggest one is winning games. They are as driven to win now as they were when they were children. Defeat is not acceptable to them and they will make sure their bodies are in the best physical shape to produce performances to win games.

434. In England the weather is obviously colder than the South American countries and hotter European countries such as Spain and Italy. In hot weather, players can not move around for as long as in England or say Germany and this has the influence on the style of football they play.

INTERNATIONAL COACHES AND PLAYERS

435. If you are a coach or a player, it's key to your development that you have an open mind. Players or coaches who think they know it all will stand still and will fall behind. It is fascinating listening to other players, coaches and managers and especially comparing notes with coaches from other countries.

436. Ajax, the great club from Holland and legendary producer of skilful creative players, encourages their scouts to never look for defenders but look for attacking players and then move them back positionally as they develop. Technical excellence is their major objective, followed by intelligence and speed. The most important player in Ajax is the link player, usually called the playmaker. A big training session focus for them is to ensure that the players work in their specialist area of the field, receiving the ball and developing repetitive passing options. When the players then come together in the team they are aware of their positional space and requirements. Many players from Holland played street football and learnt their profession through three- or four-a-side mini matches. Kids have great imagination so if they did not have a pitch to play on they created a pitch using the kerbside as goals.

There was a saying in the 1970s and 80s that if you had seen one Ajax team play you had seen them all. The style of football and the style of players in all their teams mirrored the first team. If a player in the first team was injured a 'replica' player would be brought in from the reserve team.

I have only witnessed this once in England – when I played against Brian Clough's great European Cup winning team in the late 1970s and a month later played against their reserve team. The resemblance was uncanny. The style of the players, the formation they played and the set plays were all identical to the first team.

In Brazil the culture is all about 'caressing' the ball and the warm climate encourages youngsters to develop their skills through beach football or Futsal. Most of the legendary Brazilian footballers came from lower-class backgrounds where their skills were perfected in the streets kicking around with their pals. They played with freedom and they played for hours on end. They did not receive organised coaching until they were 17 years old. They picked their own relaxed teams and this simple factor motivated them to develop their own skills to make sure they were picked first and not embarrassingly last.

Carlos Alberto Parreira, the Brazilian national coach, says that Brazilian players are not intimidated by their opponents as they are all comfortable with the ball. He says that the Brazilian style of play is to dominate ball possession and allow players the freedom to produce their skills. They allow for the creative and flair players to produce the unexpected.

Brazilian international Robinho started playing Futsal at five years old and also developed his skills playing barefoot in the streets with stones and even fruit. This activity helped give him control of the ball at a very early age. The great Pelé told him to love the game and love the ball.

Brazilian players are taught to have open minds and to learn their trade. Many of them play abroad with the Brazilian Football Federation saying that there are more than 5,000 Brazilian players playing in different countries. In 2007 alone over 1,000 Brazilian players were transferred abroad.

In Spain the great Barcelona spends millions of Euros every year to develop talent. From six to eight years old the players train with a ball each for one hour per week with internal club matches on a weekend. The players are encouraged to practise new tricks without the fear of criticism and they have are given lessons in agility and co ordination.

They play four versus four as a basic match formula where players have lots of touches of the ball and they learn to defend and attack in quick end to end action.

In Germany the giant Bayern Munich have a slightly different structure, where young coaches of 18–20 years old with a sports education take the 9–12-year-olds' training and they focus on long-term development where improvement is highly regarded and results at this stage are not. The coaches move through the age groups with the players.

The French set up their National Coaching School in Clairfontaine in 1990 and it produces a target of 20 top 15 year old players each year. The players live, train and are educated on the site and they are taught how to live the life of a top dedicated sportsman.

There was a lot of public criticism of the French football so the French Football Federation built the National Coaching School and the results over the years have been fantastic. England planned to build a similar style school in the Midlands but funding was redirected into building the new Wembley Stadium, and it did not go ahead. It is a shame as Clairfontaine has produced players who have won World and European Cups for France.

The French Arsenal Manager Arsène Wenger has a favourite saying: 'Results bring confidence and confidence brings results.'

437. England's last international success was in winning the World Cup in 1966. I believe it will be more difficult for England to win another major European or World Cup trophy in the foreseeable future as they now have so few English players playing in their own Premier League and, unlike the Brazilians, there are hardly any English internationals playing abroad. David Beckham is the only English player who has recently enjoyed success playing abroad, but who could ever have envisaged this tiny kid developing into the major world sporting superstar he is today? If anybody has used their talents to the maximum it is David. If you look at his major skills he has one outstanding feature and that is the accuracy of that magnificent right foot, which has delivered the most fantastic crosses, passes and dead ball kicks. From childhood he has perfected this skill and it has been admired by the world's top players. If you also consider that David does not possess great speed or pace, is not strong in the tackling or heading department and has a very average left foot, you have to admire his dedication and mental strength.

Can you as a young player develop that one skill that will put you at the top of your footballing profession? We are not talking about being an average multi-skilled player here, but developing and focusing on this one skill. Yes, it can be done, but you will need to spend thousands of hours to perfect it just as David Beckham has.

438. I know academy directors who have been very frustrated with both the chairman of their club and the first team manager. They have said that the chairman wants a quick fix, so instead of waiting to see a youngster mature and be good enough for the first team he allows the manager to spend money on big transfer fees and wages and does not invest enough in his club's academies.

The top experienced managers generally have a longer-term view and they want to have an input into the organisation of their academy. I know of top household name managers who will watch their academy team on a Saturday morning in front of a few spectators and then be fully charged up with their first team on the same afternoon in front of 50,000 fanatical supporters.

But I also know a number of managers who have never seen their youth team play and they only have enthusiasm for a player who the academy coach has suggested they take a look at training with the first team. This type of manager, who has changed clubs frequently, knows he could not be at this club for long so why waste his time looking at young players as he could be on the move again.

The clever clubs, with a longer-term plan, have a structure to attract all the best youngsters from an early age and they make sure they have the ongoing knowledge and contacts to pick the best players in their catchment area before their local rivals.

439. I see big clubs that have developed a fantastic academy set up over the last 10 years and have developed quality players for their first team and even sold on players they have developed for millions of pounds. These clubs will also buy proven international players and the reason they can do this is that they develop their own youngsters and every player in their first team has not cost millions of pounds in transfer fees with high wages.

Other big clubs that have not had a long-term academy strategy have lost players to the academy that has invested money. Parents see that youngsters are being given a chance in a club's first team and they want their children to go to that club's academy. The established club with a good youth system now has many international players who are good enough to play for the first team in the future or be sold for a healthy profit to fund more activity.

440. Scouts give their opinion of a player and we can all have varying opinions of what makes a good player. There are plenty of examples of players who were disregarded as having average ability but who a few years later have developed physically and mentally and now have the 'wow factor'. Being rejected can absolutely dissolve your spirit to continue or it can highly motivate you to prove people wrong.

441. I joined Manchester United as an apprentice professional at 15 years old. The previous year's intake of apprentices were mostly schoolboy internationals. They were more gifted, but some of their attitudes were appalling. As an apprentice you had certain duties to perform such as cleaning the first team players' training and match boots, making sure their kit had been washed and laid out for training and matches and cleaning the dressing rooms at the training ground or at Old Trafford. Some of the previous year's intake thought that as they had achieved international schoolboy status they had made it as a professional and that their future as a top player was secure in terms of success and financial gains.

The coaches worked very hard with them to develop their abilities and to improve their lazy attitudes and my year's intake watched as they posed and undermined our efforts. Their attitudes provided the additional motivation that drove our group forward. We spent more hours making sure the buildings were spotless and the boots were shining, and while the lazy ones were shopping or playing snooker we spent extra afternoons practising our football skills.

None of group of lazy international schoolboys played for the Manchester United first team and none of them made the grade at other professional clubs. Their abilities were good but their attitudes were flawed. In our hardworking age group, several players played first team football for Manchester United and a number went on to achieve over 50 full international caps for their respective countries and played in World Cups.

A great attitude, hard work and being a team player are the very basic skills that provide the foundation for you to build upon.

442. To see a smashing young player work hard, be dedicated to his profession and achieve success is great; however they are only in the small minority. For every one that enjoys success there are nearly 100 that do not become a professional player. Players can be rejected at any age from nine to 19 years old and as individuals we take this blow in different degrees of disappointment.

A player on a six-week trial has hardly had any time at the club, whereas a 19-year-old who has been told that he will not make it as a professional player might have spent three evenings a week training with the club since he was nine years old – over half of his life.

In my opinion I do not think clubs are great at supporting youngsters or helping them deal with this shattering decision and I see little being done by clubs to assist them in finding other professional or amateur clubs or jobs for them. It is often left up to parents, families and friends to pick up the pieces and re-motivate the youngsters to move on and make a future for them selves. Their pride has taken a jolt and no doubt some won't have seen this decision coming.

Your disappointment, though, could be another coach's joy as there are coaches and managers at a lower level that would be delighted to have you play for them. At first you could feel upset that somebody has approached you to play at a lower level of football and you might think that this is not the level you wanted to play at. But take the approach as a compliment, and understand that by playing at a lower level you would be the big fish in a smaller pond where your abilities could be seen and your confidence could again blossom. You might attract the attention of a bigger club once again. It is a fact that most players who initially join a Premier League club have to leave that club and go down a level or two before they move upward again.

STEPPING DOWN

'It could be the making of you.'

443. As a player I experienced the highs and lows in football in a very short period of time. Every player at every level loves the highs that football can bring, but playing for your childhood heroes really is a dream come true. One minute I was playing in the Manchester United first team at 17, and winning the European Youth Cup for England in Switzerland – then bang, my career was threatened by recurring ankle problems.

After 10 months out with injuries there was little chance of returning to the Red Devils' first team and once you have experienced first team football you do not want to return to the reserves. During my time out injured Manchester United bought another left-winger, a fantastic player who went on to represent England at full international level.

A number of lower-league clubs wanted me on loan but I wanted to move back to my north-east home so I chose Hartlepool United where I received a warm welcome. The facilities were a culture shock compared to my three years at Old Trafford, where everything was laid on for you. The training kit was old and had holes in it, and seemed to smell different from the fragrances used in the laundry room at Old Trafford. The dressing rooms were wooden and always cold – a match struck by accident would have caused at least 75p's worth of damage.

I can recall one match being postponed as we could not

raise a team because of illness. This was true, but the type of illness was never mentioned as it was embarrassing to all concerned at the Victoria ground. The reason was 'boils'. A number of the players, including me, had boils on various parts of our bodies which made it very difficult to walk never mind train and win matches. Mine looked like a spot on my knee and I dare not show anybody for fear of ridicule.

I could not move my knee at all and it took four days for the treatment to draw the pus from the wound. It was like squeezing toothpaste from a tube. I was one of the lucky ones as Bobby Scaife, our midfield dynamo, had a boil in let's say an uncomfortable place, which made it difficult to sit down. Boils are apparently caused by stress or bad hygiene. That was confirmed to me when I went for a drink of water in the kitchen and found a small dead shrew in the sink. I asked Harry the groundsman how it had got there and to my amazement he said he'd found it in the players' big bath! Puzzle solved.

I was a first choice player at Hartlepool and enjoyed the buzz of the 3,000-strong crowd in a small arena which provided a reasonable atmosphere. It was miles better than playing for the Manchester United reserves in front of a couple of hundred people in a stadium that held 60,000. Our results were announced on national TV at 5pm on a Saturday afternoon, our match report was seen in the *Hartlepool Mail* and the *Middlesbrough Gazette Sporting Pink* and we were live on the local radio station. It was great to see your personal match rating in the *Sunday People*, but not if you'd had a poor game. The people at Hartlepool were smashing and my confidence returned in each match even though I felt as though I had lost some of my speed due to previous injuries. Quickness was a strength of mine and it would determine which level I would play at as a professional.

After a reasonable FA Cup run I decided it would be sensible to stay at Hartlepool and use the club as a base to play well and hopefully move back up the divisions. I did just that when I joined Huddersfield Town three years later. It was good to return to my family home and move out of digs in Chorlton in Manchester, and Tommy Docherty the Manchester United manager wished me good luck. He said I was a very good professional, but we both knew my appearances in the first team shirt at Manchester United were over.

They say when you leave Manchester United you are going backwards as a professional footballer and I agree 100% with that view.

444. While players are trained and encouraged to improve their individual skills, the objective is then to bring all the best players together and to form them into a multi-skilled team. Each team member needs to know what is required of him and must then carry out this requirement.

It is important that the players gel together – if some players do not like each other it is vital that they put this aside, work together and respect each other's abilities. The players need to have the desire to be successful. Their talent and ability will not make them successful alone; it's spirit and drive that will win through. Their preparation must be thorough and they must practise until their confidence is sky high.

During their time at an academy or centre of excellence, players will be assessed as to how they perform under pressure from opposing players. A player might have a good first touch, but under pressure from a opponent it might need further improvement, or in a one-on-one dribbling and defending session an attacker could be asked to develop his skills to beat an opponent in, say, five different ways. A defender might find it easy to pass the ball without pressure but if confronted with a strapping six-foot aggressive striker he would have to use different method of passing and aggression.

REPETITION IS THE KEY

'Work hard, take risks, and you will be rewarded.'

Research has shown that top sportsmen and women had trained for at least a ten-year period and that they had all started very young.

445. If you are good enough you are old enough. Those are the words that assistant-manager Pat Crerand repeated to me as I walked down the tunnel to make my debut for Manchester United away to Manchester City in front of 51,000 ecstatic supporters. I was only 17 years of age and one of the youngest players every to play first team football for Manchester United.

I played because Manchester United is a club that gives

youngsters a chance – as long as they are good enough. Age is not a barrier to them, but ability and attitude is everything. A world-famous club needs players with a certain type of character as the expectation to win is quite a burden to carry. In addition to winning, these elite clubs also have a historical responsibility to play attractive football home and away on every occasion.

446. Parents now have a better understanding that youngsters taking scholarships at clubs need to have an academic education with the club in case the their football careers do not work out as hoped.

These players must be fully dedicated during the course of their scholarship as these could be the most important years of their lives. They must be single-minded and realise that they can't lead the same sort of social life as their non-footballing friends. While their pals can eat and drink what they want and perhaps stay up late, footballers must live their lives as athletes who are determined to go the distance and to have a career that could bring them incredible rewards. If coaches see that a player lives a good life and is always in a good physical condition then they will be given the stage to perform on. Players who love the late-night social scene will easily be found out. They will not only struggle to keep up with their dedicated colleagues in training but reports will go back to the club from members of the public. People who are supporters of the club expect you to leave an athlete's life and people who are perhaps a little jealous of your success will eagerly call the club to inform them of your timekeeping and behaviour.

Players who are that are little bit extra special will be forgiven once or even twice, but players who are just doing okay could soon be heading for the exit door.

It's a fantastic opportunity to be a professional player and I have heard many stories of players who had great ability but who liked the social scene and the drink too much. These players have come to regret their lack of discipline and dedication, especially when they see their less gifted former colleagues go on to great success.

As adults we know what teenagers can be like and we know that these can be difficult years while a youngster moves physically and mentally from being a youth to an adult. As you have experienced this stage yourself it is important that you guide your youngster through this period of their lives as they don't always see the pitfalls that could occur. Believe me, dedication and positive mental application combined with ability will take you a long way.

MAKE IT HAPPEN

'Greatness is not in where we stand but in what
direction we are moving. We must sail sometimes
with the wind and sometimes against it – but sail we
must, and not drift, nor lie at anchor.'

AUTHOR OLIVER WENDELL HOLMES

447. Youngsters who have been given this great opportunity to join a club's academy or centre of excellence must be aware of jealousy from their friends and must be focused on trying to achieve their dream.

Tell your friends how important this is to you – if they are true caring friends they will understand and support you. If they do not understand then you need to question if they are really the friends you thought they were.

'Never lose sight of your dreams. Whatever you do give it 110% or don't bother.'

448. If a player starts at an academy at nine years old and moves through to being a young professional at 18 years old he will have seen many players leave in that space of time. Over half of his life has now been spent dedicated to becoming a professional player. Still, as a young pro he is only just on the first rung of the ladder to 'making it'.

Many players celebrate their first professional contract, but few understand that they are now being treated as an adult and judged as an adult. Incredibly after all these years they are still talked about as 'having potential'. At top clubs, young players could end up training with established first team professionals who are old enough to be their dad.

You deserve congratulations for your achievements to date as you have clearly been regarded as one of the best players in your age group and in your position. What you might not realise is that the club will have a list of players in your playing position from the first team player down to the under-9s player, and the club will compare all of these players with each other to develop a long-term view.

A player who moves onwards and upwards always has a goal to achieve, an objective to go for, a plan, and they are always focused to move to the next level. They are never

satisfied with their performance levels. This is a great thing
to have in your mentality.

THE FUTURE PLAYER

'Your future is the result of your actions.'

449. The game will continue to become quicker and
developing sports science will assist players in becoming
fitter and quicker at making decisions on the field of play.
Clubs and countries who develop creative players who can
react quickly will win the trophies.

Players' dietary requirements will be further improved
upon and medical advances will return injured players to
the field a lot earlier than today. All players will need to
retain the ball in small spaces and a team with its fair share
of left- and right-footed players will provide the balanced
unit. Players will be stronger and even more athletic. Players
who have a good first touch will be in demand, as will
more skilful central defenders. There will still be a shortage
of left-footed players at all levels.

'Special players will continue to do special things at
special times' – I think of this quotation each time I see
Stephen Gerrard play for Liverpool.

CHAPTER 13

Match Day

'When tomorrow comes this day will be gone
forever. Let today be something good.'

AUTHOR UNKNOWN

If the coach and their players have worked well in training
and their planning and preparation has been of a high
standard, everybody will look forward with tremendous
enthusiasm to match day.

PRE-MATCH PREPARATION

450. So match day has arrived and everybody is looking
forward with great excitement to the match kicking off.
The coach has prepared the players in training and they
know their positions in the team and what is expected of
them. A coach will have assessed his players' strengths
before deciding on the team's formation.

In matches for the younger children the emphasis needs

to be based on 100% enjoyment with little emphasis being on winning the match, although I must say it adds to everybody's enjoyment if the team plays well and does manage to win. As long as the coach's and parents' intentions are focused on fun, there is no need to apologise for trying to win a match.

Never give your players an excuse to perform badly, as they will use it if the match goes against you. I have seen managers complaining about a long coach journey, or the state of the pitch, and when their team loses his players then also moan that they should have travelled the day before and stayed overnight, or that the pitch was not conducive to good passing. In professional football the media expect comments from the managers on a daily basis and sometimes the manager can say things that he had no need to say. His moaning can affect the players and they then have a ready-made excuse when they fail.

Make sure that you have had a good night's sleep and plenty of rest and that you are mentally and physically prepared to play and enjoy your match with great passion and enthusiasm. Deep sleep is important to the body as this is when muscles are repaired and tendons and ligaments are strengthened.

Players can have fantastic ability, but if the motivation to provide the effort is not there, their ability will be diluted and the player's performance will be very average at best.

Are your kit and boots clean? Do your boots fit well? Loose boots can give you blisters and tight boots can cause cramped toes and early arthritis. Is your bag packed with the necessary shin pads, drinks, change of clothes and toiletries?

MATCH FOOD AND DRINK

451. Eating and drinking the night before a match and also on match day is very important. Eating the correct foods and drink at this time will give you the vital fuel and energy to maximise your ability. If you do not eat and drink correctly you will not have the confidence to perform your skills, nor the stamina and drive to last a full match.

A good meal the evening before a game should include plenty of carbohydrates such as a spaghetti, a jacket potato or a large portion of baked beans on toast. Research has confirmed that a high-carbohydrate meal eaten three to four hours before a match can improve performance. If a match has a mid-morning kick-off a light breakfast of cereal or toast and jam and a banana can be taken, again with a healthy intake of two or three glasses of water. Allow two hours before a match for the snack or meal to digest.

ARRIVING AT THE GROUND

'Football matches are not usually won by the best players, but collectively by the best team.'

452. So now it is time to leave for the match. Top professional teams stay in a hotel for both home and away matches, while other teams only stay in a hotel if the away match includes a lot of travel.

Professional teams arrive at the ground about 70 minutes before kick-off as this allows them to have a look at the pitch to decide what length of studs to wear, and to acclimatise to their surroundings. It also allows them to sort out any tickets for friends and relatives and then to focus in the 'mental zone' in readiness for the match.

Players focus in many different and individual ways. Some like to listen to peaceful music on their headsets while others really like to turn up the volume and hear their favourite rock bands blast out the beat. I have known some players go into a state of near-hibernation, preferring their own lonely state, while others have jumped into a freezing cold bath or shower to awaken their senses.

If you are in a junior team, a good time to arrive is 40 minutes before kick-off as this gives you time to have a little social chat with your pals before getting changed for the match, a motivational team talk with your coach, and a good warm-up.

THE COACH

'Do what you want to do in life but do it with a passion.'

453. During the last training session before a match, the coach will have assessed all of his potential team's fitness and attitude. If his team are on a winning run he will try to leave the team unchanged or only make small changes to cope with injuries or suspensions. If the team are having a difficult time and wins are hard to come by, he will need to make changes to try and instil new enthusiasm and perhaps make some tactical changes, either to counteract the other team's strengths or to change the formation to an attacking one.

Coaches always need to have a plan B or even a plan C as unexpected events do occur such as a player feeling ill on match day or even an injury during the warm-up. I remember seeing a player at a top match posing for a photograph with his arms crossed and a foot on the ball, a typical footballer's pose, when his own player shot at goal in the pre-match warm-up and hit the player on the head. He turned the ankle which was on the ball. The player missed this match and the next six matches due to ankle ligament damage. These unexpected events do happen so contingency plans are needed just in case. The world most successful people take care of the small details, so make sure your attention to detail is complete.

'Being attentive to the minor details could have a huge impact on the major outcome'

GETTING CHANGED

'Live for the moment, live in the now and seize the opportunity.'

454. The coach has named his team for the day and the players quietly get changed and focus on their role in the team. Most top professional teams have a TV screen in the home changing rooms and they ether use it to play music or they play a motivational video to stimulate the players. The coach will experiment to see what sort of pre-match environment is best preferred and suited to his players.

Some players will be disappointed that they are not in the squad or the starting team for the match while others will start to wind themselves up into an emotional state ready to strongly compete right from the first whistle. Professional teams normally name the starting team after the previous day's training, or on the morning of the match. Junior coaches wait to see who has turned up at the agreed meeting time before selecting the team.

THE WARM-UP

455. Professional teams now tend to start the warm up 30–40 minutes before kick off. With muscle strains accounting for 44% of injuries, the warm-up is vital to prevent injury and to get the players ready for a confident performance. If they know they are well prepared they are mentally happy.

If you are going to a match it is always a good idea to go early and see the different match warm-ups. The goalkeeper is usually separated from the outfield players and will be working with the specialist goalkeeping coach and the reserve goalkeeper.

The outfield players normally work with the fitness coach and gently warm their muscles up, before doing a regimented jogging and running session which includes side-to-side running and turning, flicking their heels, and high knees. Once this low-key activity is completed the players move through a serious of quicker more intense running, gradually achieving activity at match speed.

Stretches on the key muscle groups follow, and then perhaps a small five-a-side keep possession match in a small area. There are no tackles and quick, disguised passing using one or two touches is encouraged to get their minds up to match pace. Once this is done, strikers might take some shots at the match keeper and the outfield players pass together in key groups such as defenders and midfielders.

I like to see junior teams fully warm up without the ball and then follow the professional style by gradually moving to a ball between three or four players passing over a gradually increasing distance. To sharpen them up mentally, have a player in the middle of a circle of four players. The middle man has to win the ball off the players around the circle. Warm-up time for junior players should last for 15 minutes before the match. Do not allow the referee or the other team to force you into starting a match before you are fully warmed up.

Warming your muscles forms the same principle as a car warming up. The car and our bodies work much more efficiently when our engines gradually approach working temperature.

456. After their major warm-up, professional teams will return to the changing room ten minutes before kick off and after a final briefing from the coach the teams will emerge together from the tunnel with their opponents.

On match day, the final 10 minutes before the players go out to perform is the most important time for the coach to influence the players. He has prepared the players in training so they should know their roles and responsibilities. He highlights only two priorities to each player and reminds them to visualise previous successes and how well they played on those occasions. He finally makes sure that they are now fully switched on into match mode or as some professionals call it moving into 'warrior' or 'battle' mode.

457. At this stage the players want to see the coach talking and acting positively, showing strong body language without fear. They only want to hear a couple of reminders and then they want the coach to wish them good luck. Players do not want too many instructions at this stage as it can take focus away from their key responsibilities. One of the final comments a coach will make is 'win your battles'. What he means is to win the first tackle against your matched-up opponent and show them that your early strong challenge is only a taste of things to come. Players must concentrate on every second of the game and not let their minds get ahead of them by sensing a victory too soon.

458. The final instruction to children before they go onto the field should be a simple one: go and enjoy yourself. A youngster will appreciate this comment as it frees them up to play in a more relaxed manner where there are no fears of making mistakes. The simplest instruction you can give to a junior team or a professional team is to tell them to go and score more goals than the opposition.

THE MATCH

'All for one and one for all.'

459. Do not criticise your competitors and opponents as you are handing them a great motivational tool. Professional club coaches get excited when another club gives them or their team criticism. The defending coach will often copy the offending newspaper article and put it on the team notice board, and it will be used to wind up the players. This material works and I have seen players bonding together in a highly motivated, high energy manner to 'get back' at the other team's insults. It is a much better idea to praise the other team's club, history, management and players as hearing these compliments can make them mentally relax.

460. History has shown that teams scoring the first goal have a 70% chance of going on to win the match. Starting the game knowing that 65% of goals are scored in the first third of match time should help players concentrate, as should the statistic that 34% of goals are scored from set plays, which should encourage all coaches to spend time on developing their tactics for set plays and also working on ways of defending well to stop their opponents scoring from set plays.

The top teams have skilful dribbling players who have the art of unlocking defences from wide positions and this is why a high 48% of goals come from dribbling and crossing.

461. The actions of the coach will be determined by how the match is going. Top coaches with the best players can normally sit back and trust the ability and temperament of their proven expensive players. Coaches who are struggling at the bottom end of the league table are a much more animated breed, encouraging their players to more effort. Many events can happen in a match, from scoring goals and conceding goals to players being sent off or injured and decisions going against your team.

During breaks in matches you see players taking on additional water as they fully understand the importance of water intake. They know that by having the correct level of fluid in their bodies they are able to concentrate more, especially in the very last stages of the game where fatigue due to heavy muscles and tired minds can cause errors that can lead to mistakes and as a consequence lost opportunities and lost games.

462. On my Manchester United debut against Manchester City, two players were sent off for fighting and they refused to leave the field. The referee took both teams off the field and threatened to call the match off. He went into both dressing rooms and said that if our player, Lou Macari, and their player, Mick Doyle, did not stay off the pitch he would abandon the match and 51,000 very enthusiastic fans would have to go home early – which could potentially cause trouble. All this and we hadn't reached half-time yet!

I believe that this has sort of event had never happened before in British football and it has never happened since, but it happened on my professional debut!

HALF-TIME

463. An improvement in attitude will have the biggest effect on your second-half improvement.

A coach should maintain his own and his players' desire and enthusiasm at half-time; however he does have to be careful that he does not overdo the praise as his players can lose momentum and start to believe that the second half should be just a formality. While one coach has over-praised his team, the opposing coach could be really laying down the law demanding greater effort. This could mean that one team starts the second half in an easy-going manner, in their comfort zone, while the other team treats the second half as the game of their lives.

Always challenge individual players to focus on their own tasks, and then the team to give collective effort and commitment. As the players have their half-time drink the coach of the team that's in the lead will usually tell them to just do more of the same, or a losing coach might make some changes to the formation of the team or bring some substitutes on. It is important at this time that the players receive a top up of water to energise them for the second half and stop fatigue. The hyped up players will encourage the quieter players and the coach will repeat his speech about togetherness to encourage his team.

464. Statistics show that many goals are conceded just after half-time, when there is also an increased risk of injuries. It could be that the players are still focused on the dressing room events at half-time and that their muscles have relaxed in the break. It is a good idea, therefore, to cut short the half-time break and return to the pitch a little earlier to warm up again at match pace. This will physically and mentally help your team. Seeing your team looking fully prepared can give you the mental edge.

THE LAST 30 MINUTES

'Through thick and thin – together.'

465. As the match approaches its final thirty minutes the coach will either look to re-energise his team with fresher legs, put on more defensive-minded players to keep a winning position, or put on his striking super-sub to score the decisive goal.

Top managers with big squads now try to rest key players with other important games coming up. A player could also be substituted if he has received a yellow card and the coach does not want to risk him being sent off.

466. In junior football the coach should try to make sure that all his substitutes have some match time. Some coaches will put these players on regardless of their current winning or losing position and others will just put one sub on as gesture.

At this key time in a match, physically and mentally strong players will dig deep and push their team-mates towards completing the task. These players will remain strong for the full duration of the match.

AFTER THE MATCH

467. So the final whistle blows and the players and coaches shake hands. The professional teams will return to the changing rooms to allow the supporters to leave and then they will return to the pitch to take part in the cool down. Immediately after the final whistle the players will need a litre of fluid on board to help rehydrate them.

The cool down will include jogging, sidesteps and winding down twists and turns. This light running will be followed by stretches. At this time the substitutes who have not played, and those who have only played for a short period, will have a more energetic session of running and stretches. Then it is back to the changing rooms where the coach will select his words carefully to describe his team's performance. Emotions run high before, during and after a match and if criticism is to be given it should be left to the next training session. Football is a passionate game and as human beings of any age we love to be praised, especially in front of others, but straight after a match, when we know we have made mistakes or we have underperformed, is not always the best time to be told off. Positive praise for performance and effort should be handed out and big smiles should radiate around the changing rooms.

468. In junior football the coach should take the players for a light jogging session which should include stretches. The players will then return to the changing room where they will drink more water. The coach should always say thank you and well done to all the players and win, lose or draw the players should be encouraged to smile and laugh which will motivate them to want to play in the next game.

Within an hour of the match ending both adult players and junior players will benefit from eating food such as pasta and a salad or meat with vegetables, washed down with a few glasses of water to keep the players hydrated.

DEALING WITH WINS AND DEFEATS

'Show me a good loser and I will show you a loser.'

ALAN HANSEN TALKING ABOUT
PROFESSIONAL FOOTBALLERS

469. A coach should look for the positive points and give immediate praise. There is not a lot written about dealing with wins, as winning is obviously quite easy to accept. It is important, however, to be humble when you win. You worked hard for this achievement and you and your team-mates and coaches will feel pretty good. That is fantastic for team spirit and also for individual and collective confidence.

Dealing with losing, though, can be a totally different experience, and a good coach has to keep individual and team morale high. It is good to focus on looking at your results over a long period and not have a rollercoaster ride of emotions which change by the week depending on the latest result.

Experts in any sport or business will say you can see more into an individual's personality and character when they have got beaten in contrast to when they are winning.

470. Professionals are there to WIN. That is no secret it is a fact in the hard-nosed world of sport and business. Players in league games know that they have a long season ahead and that one defeat will probably make little difference. They would start to worry, though, if they had a run of defeats and it started to become a habit.

Defeat is where a good coach shows his strength and personality. He will always praise effort and he will not allow his players' confidence to be affected. What he says and how he says it can have a positive or a negative impact on them. He must be careful after a defeat that his long-term relationship with the players, which he has developed over a period of time, is not demolished by five minutes of negativity. A good coach will even take responsibility for some defeats.

In professional football the coach is ALWAYS looking for players better than the ones he currently has in his squad and in some cases he will put up with an underperforming player until a better one is signed. But he still has to motivate the players he knows he is moving out of the club.

471. In junior football a coach can not be as ruthless as his professional counterpart and he will work to improve the players he has. Young children are encouraged to play despite the scoreline, but winning is more important to teenagers. In cup competitions and especially penalty shoot-outs the youngsters mirror the feelings of the professional players, showing despair when they miss the deciding penalty and great joy when they score the winning shot.

If your junior team is losing on a regular basis and losing heavily, it could be that the coach has made an error in putting the team into a division that is too tough for them. A call to the league secretary could help you in deciding which division to join the following season. The idea of forming a club for young people is that everybody enjoys their football and is competitive. If they can compete in Division 5 and have smiles on their faces you are winning as a junior coach, and you might now enjoy helping the lads achieve promotion to Division 4.

472. Yes, defeat can be hard to take, but it can also provide a challenge to a coach and his players. It could be that a change of formation is needed, or that a couple of enthusiastic substitutes now have the chance to show that they should be in the team. A change of training style could re-energise the players as could a change of training ground venue.

Professional teams will try a day of team bonding at the golf course or at the go-karting track, while junior players might go ten pin bowling or to the cinema together.

It is important to keep the players' morale high; however it is not always easy especially after a run of defeats. Some times a coach has to lighten up himself, get the players smiling again, and have a laugh.

473. Remember that somebody might have to motivate the coach occasionally, especially after a heavy or surprising defeat or after a run of poor results. At a professional club the Chairman or Managing Director can boost the coach, or his assistant coaches can help lift his morale. A good captain who is experienced and who is close to the coach can also put a smile back on his face.

474. The key to a good team is not how they accept winning, it is how they bounce back and recover from defeats. Look back at all the champions in any sport: the very basic foundation of their success was hard work.

'Look, no matter who wins or loses the sun's going to rise tomorrow!'

STEVE OVETT TO SEB COE JUST BEFORE THEIR 1980
SHOWDOWN IN THE OLYMPIC 800 METRES FINAL

CHAPTER 14

Winning Matches

'There is no I in team.'

WIN AS ONE

475. Five- to eight-year-olds do not understand that the only way to win football matches is if all the members of the team work hard together and play well together. It is a fantastic feeling when a team pulls together for each other and games are won, especially if your team are underdogs or have fought back from a losing position. A team of positive coaches and positive players will provide the motivation to perform on a consistent basis. Keep positive people around the players and in the team as negative ones can take energy from the group and start to erode the team spirit. Try to phase these people out of your group before they have any negative influence.

476. It is likely that a winning team has developed their skills together over a period of time and they know their team-mates strengths. It is rare that a team of strangers comes together and wins games immediately. It helps if the players like each other and socialise together and in junior football it is a bonus if the parents get along well. Although it's a team game, as a player you must first ensure that your game is good enough to achieve a place in the team, and this refers to children, youngsters and professional players. Every successful team has players who are good dribblers and can beat opponents with skill and speed. A winning team is a collection of players with a wide range of skills, who are mentally strong, work hard on the pitch, have a desire to win collectively as a team and have good tactics with the players playing in their favoured and best positions.

MIND GAMES

'Never let the body tell the mind what to do.'

477. With a team of highly motivated and well prepared individuals who work as a team, anything is achievable.

If two players have similar abilities and are both equally fit with the same match intelligence, it will be the player with the best mental toughness that wins through.

It is a good idea to listen to and read about top sports-people. In a team game, some players can have a poor day and the team can still win, but in an individual sport the player takes full responsibility for their own performance.

Imagine a top golfer on the final tee at the US Masters. He is surrounded by 35,000 people on the course and there are 1 billion people watching him on live television around the world. There are television cameras everywhere, from the airship in the sky to the 200 eager cameramen and journalists clicking away at the players' every shot and facial expression. Oh and by the way, they have to get this little white dimpled ball into the hole 460 yards away in four shots or better to win the season's first 'Major' trophy. No pressure then!

478. Many individual winners say that it is that nine inches between the ears that determines how well they are going to perform. In other words, it is how they deal with all the pressures in their minds.

Right until the whistle blows at the end of any sporting encounter the players must be positively focused every second. They cannot allow themselves to switch off. They say in football 'It only takes a second to score a goal', and that vital second can be the difference between winning the big trophy and losing it.

479. Remember the 1999 Champions League final where Manchester United beat Bayern Munich 2-1 in Barcelona. The best team on the day was certainly the German team, and in the 89th minute they led 1-0 having also hit the woodwork. However, two United goals in injury time took the trophy to Old Trafford and snatched victory from the shocked German champions.

Did Bayern Munich switch off and think the trophy

was in the bag, or did United never give up hope and wish for a little bit of luck? It was probably a combination of both.

'Thinking and visualising like a winner will make you a winner.'

PRESSURE

'When the pressure is on, good players make the right decisions at the right time. Taking responsibility for the ball while under pressure is vital, especially as you move further up the ladder.'

480. What is pressure? Pressure has different meanings for different people. Thankfully children do not feel too much pressure and should not be put into pressurised situations too early. All we want children to do is enjoy their lives, play, learn, be loved and have a fun and happy life.

A feeling of pressure comes from your mind and it is how you deal with this feeling that will determine how you perform.

Pressure to adults could come from earning a wage to provide for their families, being pressurised at work to achieve targets, looking after a poorly loved one or in some countries just finding clean water to stay alive. Pressure in football comes from trying to win a place in a team and playing well enough to stay in that team, or from a coach's point of view it comes from selecting and coaching a team to perform well and keep everybody happy.

Some players thrive on a challenge and the better the opposition the better they are hyped up to perform.

481. Pressure is a good motivator, as some find it hard to focus without this mentality. Some players actually wind themselves up into an aggressive state before every game and experienced players know the level of motivation they will require as a base for their individual performance.

If a player has not worked out how to motivate himself before a match, the coach could perhaps help with some suggestions.

482. If a player has been left out of the team or squad and has not been told why there are a few positive options they can take. One is to say nothing and simply continue to support their team on match day while working even harder to become fitter and more mentally determined to do well and regain their place when the next opportunity comes, and the other option is to speak to the coach when the right time comes up.

A person who grits their teeth and in training shows the manager what he has missed will be appreciated by the manager. He will see that the player is hurting by not being involved and his fellow coaches will feed back good reports on the player's attitude. This player will come back for additional training sessions and will be the first player on the training pitch and the last off it.

A player can perhaps work out why he has missed out, and build his confidence in the areas where perhaps the manager has noticed a fault. It is also a good thing to speak to the coach and tell them that you are determined to win back your place and quickly.

PRE-MATCH NERVES

'When tomorrow comes this day will be gone forever. Let today be something good.'

AUTHOR UNKNOWN

483. You hear of players saying after a major cup final that the match and the occasion just went by so quickly that they hardly had time to enjoy it. If you see that your players are acting a little bit differently from their normal pre-match state, it is a good idea to start the warm-up earlier and put them in a small five-a-side match. It will help them get into match mode earlier, and help them feel their touch and get into the pace of the game earlier. It is also good to start warming up before your opponents as this helps players to feel that they are more prepared than them.

Visualise previous successes and remember how good these events were for you and your team-mates. Imagine having a good game today and seeing your family cheer on your success.

RECOVERING FROM MISTAKES

484. In a match try to make your first three touches good ones, and especially your first touch. On my Manchester United debut our manager Tommy Docherty told the players to give me an early touch of the ball to settle my nerves. I can still feel the embarrassment now as the ball was pinged out to me on the left wing and I mis-controlled the simple pass as it went out for a throw-in against us. The 10,000 Manchester City fans had a great laugh at my expense. Luckily I focused on making sure my next three touches were decent ones and my confidence grew.

485. Great players make mistakes but they know that errors are part of the game and they know that a high proportion of their touches of the ball will be positive and effective ones. The other members of the team get to know each other's strengths and weaknesses and if they see a player having a difficult time it is up to them to collectively give him a boost with plenty of encouragement especially when he achieves good work.

MATCH EMOTIONS

'Football is a fun game that I take seriously.'

ROBINHO

486. Sometimes it is a good thing to hide your true emotions from your opponents. If your opponent knows what you are thinking, they have an advantage. We have all seen professional players on a football pitch who are easy to wind up. They have a reputation and opponents know that any decision against them will put them in a state of anxiety.

Opponents can easily use this to their advantage. They will try to provoke the anxious player by talking to him during the match, insulting him and by fouling him out of sight of the match officials. This highly motivated player could be a problem to his team as any reaction or retaliation could have him sent off and be suspended for a few matches. The players that have an advantage over their opponents are the quiet ones who are 100% focused, and who do not show any emotions. They do not react to any events happening on the pitch, but they are fixed on achieving their personal goal of playing well, stopping the opposition and winning the game. Even when their team score they remain in the concentration zone, showing little emotion.

More outgoing, extrovert types cannot keep their emotions hidden and although they are well disciplined, they want to show the other team that they are gladiators in a game that they are expecting to dominate and win. They put their chests forward in an action to show that their opponents are in for a challenging game. This type of player uses anger to drive them forward and if they did not have this anger they would not be motivated to perform at their best.

THE OPPOSITION

487. In professional football coaches will have had their forthcoming opposition watched on a number of occasions and especially in the match before their game. A two- to three-page document will be drawn up showing the named players in their formation with the individual players' strengths highlighted. The type of free kicks and corner kicks they use will be analysed as will any niggling indiscipline by individual players. The list will also show where the penalty kicker prefers to score his goals.

A manager will study this information and try to plan how to take advantage of any weakness. He will show his players his plan of attack and highlight a few areas showing their strengths. He will not confuse his players or make them scared of the opposition. He wants his team to focus on what they do and not what the other team does. He will ask individual players to mark specific players at set plays. All the opposition will be treated with respect whether they are the best team in the world or a team four divisions lower. No matter who you are playing, all teams have to be broken down as each match starts with the score at 0-0, with 11 players on each team and 22 legs!

AIM HIGH AND BE BOLD

'Aim high and set a high standard.'

488. If you aim for a match quality of 10 out of 10, you might achieve 8 out of 10 which would be acceptable. If you only aim for a performance level of 7 out of 10 you will probably achieve a level of only 5 out of 10 which is poor and unacceptable.

As a coach and a player set your targets and aims high. If your players are as fit as they can possibly be and they are motivated and organised you have a chance, especially when their preparation is thorough.

MATCH CONCENTRATION

489. In a 90-minute adult match statistics show that the ball is out of play or static for 30 minutes; therefore the 22 players only touch the ball for about two and a half minutes each. For the rest of the match they are making decisions. 100% concentration is vital.

It is quite easy for children to lose focus and be distracted by events happening on the touchline. At our academy we think it is important to change the type of football activity we do every ten minutes to keep the children's interest and concentration. A few also know when their parents are coming to collect them and with ten minutes to go they are virtually standing still facing the entrance to see if their parents have arrived. But this can also really motivate some players as they want to please Mum and Dad with the effort they are giving and the success that they are achieving. Quite naturally they are looking for parental approval in addition to the coach's praise.

Older youngsters and professional players can learn to concentrate through the correct training and repetition. Good concentration is crucial to a winning objective and with practise it can be turned into a habit. You hear commentators on TV say 'The defender lost concentration and allowed the attacker to get in front of him to head in the winner.'

THE WINNING TEAM

'Everything is possible, it is just a question of working out how.'

490. Simple statistics show that in all levels of football, from World Cup–winning teams to junior teams, the team that has the most possession of the ball wins the game. As they say, you can't score goals or win matches if the other team has the ball.

Once you have the ball you have to have a lot of shots at goal. The ratios prove that the more shots at goal you create, the more chance you have of scoring.

Your team's work rate must be higher than the opposition's and your players must be fitter to ensure that when they attack at speed there are more players available to score. Additionally the fittest team will be in a better position to regain quick possession of the ball especially in their opponents' defensive areas.

Top coaches are aware that successful teams enjoy a lot of success from set plays. They practise free kicks from all areas of the pitch, and particularly in attacking areas, ensuring that all players know their part as either attackers of the ball or decoy runners.

The best teams also have great flair and creative players that can open up defences with their attractive skills. They have a great work ethic, they know their positions well, and the coaches encourage them to show their individual ability within the team structure. They are disciplined, and they believe in the system that has brought them previous success.

491. Many hours are spent on the training grounds to perfect these requirements and repetition is the key. Practise, practise and practise, repetition, repetition, repetition – and when you have done all of that, do it again and again.

When you saw the great English rugby union stand–off

Jonny Wilkinson score the winning drop-kick in the 2003 World Cup final, you probably thought how easy it looked to him. What we obviously did not see was the repetitive practise that took place to achieve the technique that would make him world famous. He practised his kicks thousands of times and he was very demanding of himself. His attention to detail was precise, as was his mental dedication to get his skill spot-on even under pressure. He prepared just in case the day came when he might have to deliver on the world stage. And Jonny Wilkinson indeed delivered in the last seconds of a World Cup final to win the trophy for England.

In cup finals players can think that these great occasions will happen time and time again for them. For some players that is the case, but for the majority it could a one-off final and their team may not achieve that level of success again. The coach will put the match into perspective by telling them that this is a big opportunity for them and that they must recognise this and grab the opportunity with both hands.

'Make the most of every opportunity; your destiny is the result of your actions.'

CHAPTER 15

Football Agents

Football agents play a very important role in professional football from the very top of the game to the lower levels. A player's agent looking after top players will have an extensive list of items to negotiate such as salary, a signing-on fee, image rights, relocation money, accommodation, cars, appearance fees, club bonuses for wins and draws and for winning competitions, loyalty money, length of contract, flights and additional bonuses for clean sheets or goals scored.

FOOTBALL AGENTS

492. Most players in the top divisions around the world have a licensed players' agent to represent them. For a number of years the rules put in place by a country's football association were only loosely adhered to; however the laws and regulations have now been thankfully adjusted to ensure that clubs, players and agents strictly abide by the rules.

Initially an agent will hear from a club, a player, a scout or just on the football grapevine that a youngster has potential. It will depend on which category of ability the player is in as to how many players' agents will try to encourage the player's parents to sign with them.

I have seen potentially big players wanted by many agents who promise to look after their youngster, but when that youngster has not fulfilled their potential or has become injured, the agent has phased himself quietly out of the player's life.

At professional level football is a big business and some agents are looking for that big payday, looking at representing the most highly-paid players and picking up a big commission. Many other agents have other businesses out of football but love the game, want to be involved and are obviously interested in making money.

493. If a player in professional football does not have an agent there is a risk that he will not achieve the salary and contract terms that a player with a licensed agent will achieve. An agent will know the going rate for a player at all levels while understanding that a striker at any level will obviously earn a lot more than a full-back at that level. There is always a shortage of goalscorers at all levels so strikers will always earn the top money at a club. They deserve this extra money as they have the most difficult job in football – putting the ball in the back of the net.

494. When a player signs a scholarship with a club his salary is generally very low to begin with and I believe that is a good thing. At this stage the player should be focusing on everyday improvement and not playing for money. In most cases during the scholarship a parent is still paying for their son's clothes, travel, pocket money and normal day-to-day expenses.

495. The big danger point is when a youngster at a big club is offered a full professional contract and moves from his scholarship money to much more significant terms. I have seen careers destroyed at this point, because the youngster is now flooded with cash which he is not used to and he thinks that he has now 'made it'. How wrong they are. They have only just arrived on one of the lower rungs of the ladder to success.

496. A group of four 18-year-olds signed full professional contracts on the same day and were paraded as the 'future' of the club. These players had agents who assisted them with their contracts. In the following year, problems arose with all four youngsters. One of these players was a less gifted one who had a fantastic attitude, but he sustained an injury.

All of the players were staying in the club's hostel and were brilliantly looked after by the owners of the hostel, who treated all the players like a great mum and dad should. Two of these players now wanted their own apartments, and new cars. Their new-found money turned their heads and they lost the dedication, desire and commitment that had helped them to achieve a professional contract. A term used in football is 'big time Charlies' and football is littered with players like this who have lost the edge and the love of simply enjoying football. Both players soon left this club with a couple of years remaining on their contracts and initially joined clubs three divisions lower, but it did not last long. One player left football through injury and the other one developed such a bad, lazy reputation that no professional club wanted him. Another one of the four couldn't handle the pressure of playing at this level and he ended up suffering from depression. In his mid-20s, he is still playing professional football.

Where were the parents and families of these players and where was the agent when these players most needed them? As I said previously, one of the four was a less gifted player who had sustained an injury. I signed him up and now he is team captain in a club which is suited to him. He has enjoyed two promotions and the management and fans really like him. He is fantastically dedicated player, who all the players look up to. He leads by example and is a great team man. During my time as an agent I have never taken a penny from the player and I remain very proud of him today.

497. The father of a young player who was in his final year of his scholarship at a Championship club asked me to represent his son. He was concerned that his son was not being treated fairly in terms of the salary he was receiving compared with the praise he was receiving from all of the coaches including the first team manager. The club were paying him £100 per week and paying for his lodgings and food at a club recommended hostel, which cost £65 per week.

The first team manager was not keen for him to have an agent, but his father was happy for me to renegotiate his contract. After a meeting the manager reluctantly agreed to move the player's salary from £100 per week to £600 per week, a huge increase. I did not ask for an agent's fee from either the player or the club. This smashing young man was now earning sensible money and he went on to enjoy his football in the Scottish Premier Division.

498. Football fans believe that all football players are living a life of luxury off the field but many in the lower divisions of the Football League in England and Scotland are barely making a living. Some regular first team players are earning less than £300 per week, which would surprise their supporters. Players in the lower divisions travel many miles from their homes to training every day and the only way they can financially do this is to car share with their team-mates.

499. Players do need to have somebody that they can trust to help them and clubs obviously try to get players for a lower salary. A player or his family does not know the going salary rate for a player in each division, but that player's agent does, and the clubs are wary of agents because they know they are informed.

500. Managers call me for information on players. They want to know if a particular player is available for transfer, how long his contract has to go, what his current salary and terms are, whether he could be for sale and whether I believe he would join their club. It happens all the time. Not many agents are former players so as a former professional player my views on a player are respected.

501. As we know, about 98% of youngsters who join a high level club will leave that club without making their first team debut. Where do they go? Do they need an agent? And would an agent want to represent them?

These players will hopefully be picked up by a lower division club than the one they are leaving, and if that happens they will be given a very average wage until they prove themselves at that level. If they prove themselves with consistent performances then they have a chance of earning a higher salary and a longer contract.

An agent can be useful when a player has been told he is not wanted and no clubs have come immediately in for him. But it could take an agent many hours trying to fix it for another club to take the player. The agent will be thinking 'What am I going to make financially for all the hours I spend helping the player achieve another contract?' At this stage a player needs an agent, but I believe that a player who is struggling to find a club should have to do most of the work and he should be the one writing letters and calling clubs asking for a trial. If he does this, an agent can then negotiate his financial terms on his behalf.

If an agent had too many of these players on his books

he would go financially bust as most of his time would be spent trying to fix these players up with clubs. If a player is invited for a trial he must be 100% match fit and mentally ready to earn a contract.

502. When clubs release young players there is rarely help from that club to find the player another club or suitable employment. There is no one waiting to assist the youngster to find a club.

A player may have been with a club since he was eight years old, but in a cold official
letter his contract can be terminated in seconds and his dream ended. I believe that the top clubs should either help players find employment or another club, or that they should pay a company or an agent a fee to help a player they have dismissed. It happens in big businesses and football is a big business.

503. Some managers will take foreign players into their clubs but others, especially the managers in the lower leagues, will not touch them with a bargepole. Their biggest question is how the player will perform when the weather gets tough in winter and whether the player will settle in a new country, a new culture and in a new weather system.

As lower clubs have a very limited financial budget they have to be sure that every player they sign will deliver the goods on the pitch. They do not have the luxury of buying a player who could 'do it for them'. They have to be sure.

I have see managers who have taken a very big risk at a

lower level and signed players on a recommendation, incredibly from somebody that they did not know that well. Both managers paid for this poor decision when the players did not perform and the manager was sacked.

504. Managers and chairmen are pressurised by supporters to spend, spend, spend and some will go beyond their common sense principles and spend money to achieve promotion to the next division.

I spoke to a chairman of a Championship big city club in 2001 and when I gave him the details of a quality foreign player he immediately, but politely, said 'no thank you'. He went on to say that his club had been let down by a foreign player in the recent past and he wouldn't be taking any more. He said his wage maximum for a player was £4,000 per week and he would not break that rule. Eighteen months later his club were promoted to the English Premier League and they panicked, bought a foreign player and gave him a three-year contract on £40,000 per week.

This club stayed in the Premier League for two seasons and then went into freefall, tumbling down the divisions. They had to move out their big earners quickly and as consequence they are now in a very difficult financial position, in a lower division.

505. I took my Players' Agent licence in 1999 at the Football Association in London. I sat an examination and then had a verbal interview. I was very pleased to pass and within a few weeks I had arranged meetings with managers, chief scouts and the chairman of clubs. It was not long after that I brought players from France on trial and three signed for a big city Championship club. I was spending many hours travelling to see matches and players and spending time in airports waiting to collect many young foreign players and take them for trials at English clubs.

The next venture put my life and the life of the trialists at risk. I collected a two French 17-year-olds from John Lennon Airport in Liverpool and brought them cross-country to Sunderland for a week's trial. They both did okay but were rejected by Sunderland as they were no better than the players they already had – a familiar statement in football.

I collected them in Sunderland but the weather worsened as we drove over the A66 on the Yorkshire/Cumbria border. At first we saw beautiful green scenery and rolling countryside but within a very short time we were driving on a few inches of snow. Fifteen minutes later that had turned into five inches of packed snow. It was becoming difficult to distinguish between the road and the fields. I was nervous but the faces on the two French youngsters showed utter horror. In very difficult circumstances I delivered them to Liverpool for their flights back to Paris.

I remember collecting two young players from Greece at Manchester Airport and taking them to Manchester City for a trial game. I asked them what the weather in Greece was like when they left and they said it was 28 degrees and wall-to-wall sunshine. Their trial match took place the following day on a very cold and rainy Manchester morning, and they totally looked out of place. They were so numb with the cold I felt sad for them, but I was happy when they enthusiastically boarded the flight home the following day. The cost of their flights, accommodation and my time and travel cost me nearly £1,000 and I promised myself never to take great recommendations from people again without having seen the player first. The players were great lads but their level of ability was miles away from Manchester City's standards.

506. Jacques Santini, the former French Manager was an interesting one. I received a call from a French agent who I knew well, who said to me that Jacques was coming to the end of his contract and if the French Federation were not going to renew his contract he would be interested in coming to manage in England. France at that time were second only to Brazil in the world rankings and Santini had proven to be a very successful club manager in France.

When I called several of the top English clubs who were rumoured to be looking to change their manager I was very surprised when two of the chairmen I spoke to said they had no idea who Santini was. I explained his current position as the French national team's manager and his successful history as a coach and they said they did not want a foreign manager. Both of these clubs were relegated from the Premier League the following season.

Another of the clubs that told me they had no interest in signing Santini was Tottenham Hotspur. I decided that the best course of action was to put together a marketing plan to promote Santini in England. I contacted a very well respected and experienced English sports journalist called Bob Cass and invited him to come to Paris with me to interview Santini at the French Federation offices. Bob invited his colleague Daniel King to join us to interpret for us as Santini spoke little English. A photographer joined us from London and after a three-hour meeting we had a great article, backed up with photographs of us and Santini with the Eiffel tower in the background.

I called Sky Sports and they came to Paris the following week and again interviewed Santini. Within days everybody in England was talking about Jacques Santini and when he was coming to manage in England. He did get his wish to manage Spurs – Daniel Levi, the Tottenham chairman, signed him within weeks of the national press and TV coverage.

Author's Note

I enjoy my unique life in football, especially coaching the fantastic children at my football academy. If you have an interesting sporting story to tell me, or a funny, happy or unusual moment in junior football, you are welcome to contact me and I might even put your story in a book.

If you would also like advice about being a players' agent then I can be contacted on p.bielby@btinternet.com

'Proud to be the son of my father and proud to be the father of my son and daughter.'